BEYOND THE RUINS

FIVOS PANAYIOTOU

Published by MMH Press, 2021
Copyright © 2021 Fivos Panayiotou
Cover & Interior design by Chelsea Wilcox

All rights reserved. No part of this book may be used or reproduced by any means, graphic, electronic, or mechanical, including photocopying, recording, taping or by any information storage retrieval system without the written permission of the copyright owner except in the case of brief quotations embodied in critical articles and reviews.

Some scenes in this book are based on true events. Some events may have been compressed, and some dialogue has been recreated. The author has gone to great lengths to ensure that all identities are protected by changing the names and claims his rights to share his story to help others.

Because of the dynamic nature of the Internet, any web addresses or links contained in this book may have changed since publication and may no longer be valid. The views expressed in this work are solely those of the authors and do not necessarily reflect the views of the publisher and the publisher hereby disclaims any responsibility for them.

 A catalogue record for this work is available from the National Library of Australia

National Library of Australia Catalogue-in-Publication data:
Beyond the Ruins/Fivos Panayiotou

ISBN: 978-0-6451484-7-3 (Paperback)
ISBN: 978-0-6451484-8-0-9 (Ebook)

"Knowing yourself is the beginning of all wisdom."
—Aristotle

DEDICATION

This book is dedicated to my Yiayia, for always backing me.
—Fivos Panayiotou

FOREWORD

Based on a true story, this remarkable body of work by Fivos Panayiotou explores the challenges a Greek Cypriot refugee faces growing up in Australia in the '80s as a result of failed peace talks between Greece and Turkey since the 1974 invasion. His journey is one that comes to test the very core of his identity as he comes under fire in a new land. Riveting and unputdownable, Panayiotou tackles the hard subjects of bullying, racism and identity politics, as well as explores the pain of abandonment and betrayal, revenge, intergenerational trauma, and the healing the power love and forgiveness as he struggles to find himself in his life. This deeply moving coming of age story is ultimately one of survival though, as Panayiotou bravely and candidly shares his accounts of psychic torment and loss, through the pain of loss of country, loss of identity, loss of family, and loss of himself. In this book there flows a river of eternal strength—not to mention something we can all learn from—when we dare to look *Beyond the Ruins*.

—Susan Wakefield, Developmental Editor

Contents

CHAPTER ONE: Every Cypress Tree Has Its Roots 1
CHAPTER TWO: A New Start 15
CHAPTER THREE: Alora 23
CHAPTER FOUR: A Divided Land 36
CHAPTER FIVE: Broken 48
CHAPTER SIX: An Australian Christmas 56
CHAPTER SEVEN: Sick Days 63
CHAPTER EIGHT: Opa! 73
CHAPTER NINE: Bully for You 82
CHAPTER TEN: Run for Your Life 94
CHAPTER ELEVEN: Karate Kicks 104
CHAPTER TWELVE: Sixteen Candles 117
CHAPTER THIRTEEN: Oh, Baby 128
CHAPTER FOURTEEN: Where the Wind Blows 138
CHAPTER FIFTEEN: A Pregnant Pause 152
CHAPTER SIXTEEN: The Dawn of a New Era 163
CHAPTER SEVENTEEN: Beauty and the Beast 175
CHAPTER EIGHTEEN: Beyond the Ruins 185
EPILOGUE: After the End 194

CHAPTER ONE

Every Cypress Tree Has Its Roots

Apollo Mazarou sat by his bedside rubbing two mittened palms together; it was a cold and drizzly night and unusual weather for Cyprus, especially around this time of year, which normally saw hot and humid days melting into balmy nights. The Greek island nation was known for its perfect, year-round weather and tropical climes, so the current conditions were less than favourable and certainly far from the norm. But nothing seemed normal tonight, and Apollo felt the weight of change bearing down on his shoulders; no, Apollo had much bigger things on his mind, given that, come morning, he and his family would be making the arduous journey halfway around the world to Australia. His last night in this place he had always called home, Apollo felt a sudden wave of sadness wash over him; the thought of saying goodbye not just to his home but his entire country felt like a monumental earth shift, an earthquake so great he might just fall down in between the cracks and lose himself. Not to mention the fact that he was feeling more than a little apprehensive about the unknown and wondering what awaited him on the other side of the world in a new and foreign land he knew nothing about.

Apollo was just twelve years of age when his father, Mateus, had announced that the family would be leaving their homeland of Cyprus, bound for Australia. The year was 1986, and Mateus had been struggling to find work as a steel fabricator ever since the 1974 invasion took place. Mateus and his wife Mary eventually decided that it was better to go to Australia where there were many more opportunities for work and the promise of being able to make a life for themselves and their young family in tow. Besides, Mary's parents, Frank and Angela, were already living there; they too had had no choice but to emigrate to Australia right after the war broke out after they had all lost their homes and farms. Now Mateus and Mary were soon to follow because Cyprus offered them little to nothing; there was no work in Cyprus after the invasion, and in the aftermath, and after all that had taken place in the last twelve years they simply had to go where the work was—even if that place was fifteen thousand miles away from all they'd ever known.

Apollo lay back on his childhood bed thinking about the friends at school he'd had to say goodbye to earlier that day, especially his best friend, Massimo Ianello.

"I have no body, and I hear without ears and speak without a mouth; I can't be seen but come alive with the wind ... what am I?" Massimo asked him, grinning.

"An echo, echo, e-c-h-o!" Apollo replied, and they both laughed. Massimo was a natural prankster, and it had been a private joke the boys had both shared as two nervous school kids arriving on their first day of school. It had solidified their friendship from day one, and they'd been steadfast friends ever since, which was why it hurt Apollo to have to say goodbye.

"Hey, don't forget me, bro—you, me and Troy, we're the kings of Limassol!" Massimo reminded Apollo. "Just remember me, I will always be your friend, I am like the wind."

In search of comfort, Apollo climbed into his bed and pulled out his favourite book to read: *The Count of Monte Cristo*. He could relate to Edmund Dantès, the protagonist, who, despite being wrongfully imprisoned and betrayed by those he loved, continued to believe in God, because God never left him. When Dantès finally became successful, he got his vengeance on the world, prevailed and won—proof that the good guy always wins ... you just have to have hope and wait, he thought. Apollo closed his eyes and thought to pray—he hoped he could be strong like Dantès and make friends in this new country; books had always been his friends too, they just had a way of bringing him a sense of peace at a time when everything felt upside down and inside out. Reading helped too, to take his mind off all the things that were troubling him. Apollo loved to escape into books; it was another land filled with wonder and surprise, and it was far less daunting than what actually faced him now—escaping to a foreign land in real life, which didn't feel like much fun at all. Already Apollo could feel himself becoming nervous about going to a new country with no friends and very few family there to surround himself with. Why couldn't he just stay here with his school and his friends, a place where everything felt familiar, felt like home? He didn't want to be uprooted ... not now, not when everything finally seemed to be going right for him. He was a good kid at school, had a handful of friends, always did his homework on time and loved making baklava with his mother on the weekends. Life was comfortable, and Cyprus was home.

Eventually, Apollo drifted off to sleep, still clutching his book as he usually did, and when he awoke the next morning all of the family's belongings had already been neatly boxed. The night before his parents had taken care of all the packing, figuring it was easier after the children had gone to bed, and now their home was no longer a home but a series of rooms with boxes lined up against the walls, some with arrows pointing upwards marked 'fragile.' *Just like how I feel right about now,* Apollo thought gloomily. In fact, their home had been given to Mateus' cousins, who would move in and take care of the place in the meantime while they were gone. Apollo couldn't even bring himself to think that his bedroom would no longer be his, but his cousin's—it was just too depressing to think of. Just then, Apollo's younger brother Troy came into the bedroom carrying a suitcase; he plonked it down and sat down briefly, looking nervously out the window.

"Will we like Australia?" Troy asked, his little Greek voice quivering as he spoke. Apollo looked down at his younger brother and shrugged his shoulders. They were only two years apart in age, and you could tell they were brothers by their striking features; both had hazel green eyes and prominent Greek noses befitting their native heritage. Black Greek hair fell over their smooth olive complexions and were a testament to island life and the Mediterranean diet they lived on of home grown olives, garlic, lemon and the freshest, sweetest, most succulent tomatoes.

"I don't know—" Apollo countered, "Will Australia like us?" he shot back at his brother with a questioning look, then allowed his thoughts to drift off with the clouds.

The boys didn't have much time to chat, as their mother Mary came in and told them Uncle Peter was waiting out the front ready to drive them to the airport, and they needed to hurry to make sure they got to their flight on time. The boys were sad but they headed out the door, dragging their feet as they went. Mateus was already out the front waiting with their luggage when the boys followed their mother outside; Mary was just that type of woman, a Greek goddess who naturally drew men into following her by the sway and sashay of her hips until they literally fell at her feet. Mateus held both suitcases out for his brother Peter to take, his head held low. No words needed to be said between the two men, for the empty silence hanging between them spoke volumes. Mateus wondered when he would ever see his brother, or this house, again.

"Goodbye oikos, my home," Troy mumbled, tears welling in his eyes. Apollo followed his brother, climbing into the back seat of Uncle Peter's car, daring to look back one last time at the humble abode and its whitewashed walls gleaming in the morning sun. The flight was for eleven o'clock and they needed to get to the airport; if they made it by 11am, they'd have just half an hour to spare so that Apollo and Troy could play their favourite video games, *Frogger* and *Space Invaders,* in the arcade section before it was time to board the aircraft. Before long, their father came to grab them, and they made their way to the terminal. They boarded the plane and the friendly flight attendant smiled as she put his bag in the overhead compartment, but Apollo couldn't find anything to smile about, so, being the good Greek boy he was, he did what he was told and sat down in his seat and fastened his seatbelt. Troy was having trouble putting his bag away and started complaining to Mateus about wanting the window seat, still frustrated that he hadn't gotten to finish his video game back in the terminal. Mateus managed to distract Troy by reminding his son that he was now on a big jumbo jet, the largest aircraft carrier in the world—and how exciting their voyage would be, flying thousands of miles around the world to an island, a country they'd never seen. Apollo, however, was unconvinced by his father's promises and instead picked up the safety guide in the seat pocket in front of him. They were flying with Singapore Airlines, and this would be their third flight ever; the boys had travelled to England, Crete and the Greek islands some years earlier on vacation when they were just toddlers, but they had barely any memory of it, and this was different—because this time it was a one-way ticket with no return.

As the plane took off both Apollo and Troy clamoured in their seats to see Cyprus shrinking from the sky; they could just make out the tops of the tranquil villages below lining sun-kissed beaches and secluded bays, while inland lay the Troodos mountain region and fertile valleys; if they looked hard enough, their father said, pointing below, they would be able to see all of Cyprus' many ruins. Indeed, the island life was said to be so beautiful that it had been the birthplace of Aphrodite, goddess of love, beauty and fertility.

"In fact, legend has it that she rose out of the foam or 'afros' near the town of Paphos, which is now called Aphrodite beach—that's why Cyprus is called the island of love," Mateus said solemnly, "and that was why Marc Anthony once gave the island to his beloved Cleopatra as a gift—as a symbol of his love for her."

"What is fertility, Papa?" Troy asked innocently.

"Well, it means a place where things can grow, like a garden—where women can have beautiful healthy babies, just like you and your brother," Mateus said, smiling and looking over at his wife.

"Is that why you call Mama a goddess, too?"

"Yes son, yes—your Mama is a goddess too," Mateus said, trying not to laugh.

"So Mama's belly is a garden where I grew?"

"Exactly—"

"And are there gardens where we're going?"

"Oh yes, many, many beautiful gardens ..."

"So I can grow there too?"

"Yes, son, yes ..."

The boys continued to look out the window at the ruins, listening intently to their father as he spoke, all the while glued to the magnificent views below. Cyprus was slowly shrinking out of sight; soon it would become nothing more than a distant memory as the plane climbed higher in the sky. The international flight was twenty-two hours in all; thankfully for Mary and Mateus, the boys slept most of the way, only stirring when the cabin lights came on announcing food service. They would touch down first in Dubai, then again in Singapore for refuelling before finally landing in Sydney around dawn. The boys rubbed sleepy eyes as they moved through customs and found their way onto the last connecting flight to Melbourne, the last leg of their journey. On a warm January morning, Mary's parents, Frank and Angela Pistakis, eagerly awaited their arrival at Tullamarine airport with the promise of being reunited with their long-lost family they hadn't seen in years. Mary spotted them immediately as they exited through the large glass security doors.

"Mama!" Mary yelled and ran into her parents' arms for a long embrace. Time and distance had aged Frank and Angela, and Mary held their frail bodies close; there was so much to say, but right now no words would come; it was just pure joy to finally be reunited. Angela's eyes welled with tears as she held her daughter, then her sights set on her two precious grandchildren. The last time she had seen Apollo and Troy, they had been mere toddlers running around and barely out of diapers.

"Oh, Mama!" Angela exclaimed, repeatedly clapping her hands together. Apollo was used to this; growing up in Greece, he knew how expressive Greek women were and how much they said with their hands. Troy had no memory whatsoever of his grandmother, but Apollo had been just old enough when Yiayia had left Cyprus that his mind could reach back in time and conjure images of her from the past. He remembered Yiayia then, and he only had to study her for a moment before the memories came flooding back. There she was, hanging laundry out on the line next to whitewashed walls under electric blue Cyprian skies when Apollo was just a toddler; she still looked the same as she had back then too and hadn't aged a bit with her jet black hair tied back neatly in a bun and her smooth olive complexion, looking forever young and fresh and alive. Yiayia had certainly aged well, which Apollo had noticed was hardly at all. That good Greek complexion was genetic, it seemed, for his mother hardly looked a day over twenty, either. Yiayia's warm, smiling brown eyes met his then, and she opened her arms out wide.

"My little boureki mou! Look how much you've grown!" Angela cried out, overwhelmed with pride. Troy ran to her open arms first, while Mateus shook hands with his father-in-law, and Frank pulled him in for a bear hug.

"Right," Angela said, gesturing Frank to pick up the boys' bags, "Let's go get the car and take you to your new home; we have so much to catch up on! I've already set up a room for the boys—you must be tired after your long plane ride, so I tell you what: Yiayia is going to make you some lunch, and then we can all take a nap."

Coburg, an inner city suburb that sat in the north-west suburbs of Melbourne, was about to become their new home. It was a 1980s triple front brick home and quite large; in fact the six bedroom property often felt too grand and sparse for a little retired couple. Frank had had enough money saved before the war of 1974 and had managed to get to Australia with most of it intact; in the past decade, his business in Melbourne had also done well, well enough for him to sit comfortably and enjoy an early retirement.

"Wow! Is this where you live, Papou?" Apollo exclaimed, wide-eyed, to which his grandfather replied with a joyful, "Yes, yes, Apollo mou—this is where Yiayia and I have lived since we left Cyprus—and now it is your home, too." The boys were so excited that they had such a spacious and nice new home environment to live in that they immediately ran through the house and out the back door to explore the large suburban garden and park surrounds the house backed onto. It was a far cry from the small abode they had called home back in Cyprus, and the sheer space was overwhelming. Frank and Angela continued to walk Mary and Mateus through the house, showing them to their bedroom and the boys' rooms down the hall.

"Wow, you really set everything up for us nicely," Mateus said feeling grateful and thanking his in-laws, and Angela playfully nudged her son-in-law in the ribs, beaming with delight and joy that they were finally, finally reunited after all these years. Of course, Frank and Angela had made several trips back to Cyprus in the past decade, but these had been short visits at best, and it just hadn't been the same as it was now because now they could all finally, really be together again.

"Ten years has been too long, my son … too long …" she said, shaking her head and fighting back more tears. "But now—now you are finally safe and here with us; and we are family after all, and this is what we Greeks do best—we stick together. Now, come get settled, and I will make us a big, healthy Greek salad and some of my famous avyolemoni egg and lemon soup with rice—and if you're lucky I will even make you some baklava for dessert because I know how much you have missed Yiayia's great cooking!" she said and laughed. Mateus rubbed his hungry belly in response and smiled, suddenly realising he was ravenous after twenty-four hours of plane food. Mary looked out beyond the kitchen window just then to the backyard and its large lemon tree, just in time to see her son climbing its branches, reaching up and helping himself to the abundant ripe lemons. Mary let go a contented sigh. This was their new life now, and she was grateful that it was beginning to feel like her new home away from home; it would just take a while to settle in, she thought.

"Mama, I brought you something special from back home, one of your favourite things," Mary suddenly declared, remembering the package waiting in her bag. She pulled it out and handed it to Yiayia. "Just a little something from Mateus and I, to thank you and Papou for all you are doing to help us."

Yiayia took the package and opened it; was her favourite, Commandaria, a dessert wine known for its unique aroma and flavour and grown only on the island of Cyprus. It was recognised as the world's oldest named wine, and it dated back some 5000 years.

"Oh, my ormofo kouklo, you shouldn't have! This is too special! We must enjoy this after our lunch," Yiayia said as she began putting out plates of halloumi cheese and Cyprus meze, which Apollo and Troy immediately dived into like shipwrecked scavengers.

"Siga! Siga! Slowly, slowly," Mary scolded her boys, reminding them to show their manners at the dinner table. They sat in the shade under a large outdoor pergola covered in vines, and Yiayia commented that they always ate alfresco in the summer months because it felt just like being back in their homeland. Cyprus was well known for its hospitality, a fact reflected in the Greek word 'xenos,' which, translated, was used to welcome both strangers and guests alike—because the Cypriots were always a welcoming people who loved nothing more than to be surrounded by family and friends. Once the meal was over, the boys returned to playing out in the warm January sunshine while the adults caught up on all the news to be shared from home and away. Mateus told Frank how Cyprus was under extreme political upheaval as more and more people were now being forcibly displaced and losing their homes—in the hundreds of thousands, to be more exact—and the island had become more divided than ever in the wake of supercharged political divide and failed peace talks between the Greeks and Turks.

"The Turks have completely seized the northern third of the island now, Frank—and it's forced many Greek Cypriot refugees to flee to the south—given that, until fairly recently, most of these people had lived from their land. Now, they are lost and suffering, all finding themselves stranded and without jobs. It's a mess," Mateus said, drowning his sorrows in the sweet wine.

"We are the lucky ones," Frank finally said, scratching his balding temple. "Thank God we got out when we did—we know that others were not so lucky. Australia is a good country, son; just be prepared to put your head down and work hard, and you will settle here and make a good life here for yourself and your family. And just remember that Rome—or Greece for that matter—wasn't built in a day."

Mateus nodded quietly; Frank was right. He had to work hard now for his young family, and he was ready to do it—he had to do it. Just then the boys came running inside, yelling about a bird they had seen in the tree that made a funny squawking sound; it seemed to be laughing at them.

"That's called a Kookaburra, and they're laughing alright! Funny birds they have here in Australia, and so many varieties of them, too. See? They are so happy here Down Under that even the animals laugh!!" Frank laughed, then attempted to mimic their raucous cackle. The boys laughed too. Papou was sooo funny.

"Time for you boys to go get cleaned up and Yiayia will read you a bedtime story tonight," Yiayia said with a wink and a smile. The boys obeyed their grandmother and ran for the bathtub that was already filling with water. After bathtime was over, the boys settled in to their new rooms; Frank and Angela had everything set up for them and their school orientation was already planned for the coming days as well, since in Australia school resumed in early February, towards the end of the Australian summer.

"Yiayia, it's so different here, and I want to ask lots of questions," little Troy piped up. She could see the little boy's brain whizzing about.

"You can ask Yiayia anything, anytime," she said warmly, "but, for now, it is bedtime, so you get just one question before I tuck you into bed for storytime."

"Well, what Apollo and I both want to know is: why there is a blue and white ribbon tied on the lemon tree?"

"Oh, that," Yiayia explained, "That is a Greek tradition; it is believed that, if you tie something belonging to that person on a tree it will bring good luck—it will make infertile women have babies, and people will return to their loved ones. So you see, it works—because now you are finally home, here with me."

The boys both sat upright in their beds and hugged their grandmother tight; even though everything felt strange and foreign and new, something felt right, too.

"Right—into bed, and Yiayia will tell you stories of her childhood," she said, turning down the light. "Do you know why Cyprus has so many cats? Well, I will tell you the story; it goes like this: once upon a time, Cyprus was not called Cyprus at all but another name; it was called Ophiussa, which meant 'the abode of the snakes'—because the island was teeming with snakes; in fact it was overrun by them. Legend has it that an entire shipload of cats was sent to devour the poisonous snakes as a way of getting rid of them! The plan worked, because today there are hardly any snakes left; but now the problem is that there are more cats on the island than there are people! The oldest cat in the world was also discovered to have lived on Cyprus, nearly nine thousand years ago! And although your Yiayia grew up in a poor family, she loved cats—and she had many. I am sure you remember seeing a lot of cats in the village where you lived, and I will tell you many more stories about your Yiayia growing up there; they are stories of someone who grew up poor, but she never gave up on being the person she wanted to be—and you will do the same. There will be hard moments in your life, and you will have to face hard things like you have just had to do, but, just like Yiayia, you will never give up, because you are a descendant of true Greek Cypriots—and we never, ever give up! Now, time to go to sleep, because tomorrow we have another busy and exciting day planned—tomorrow you will finally get to see your new school for the first time—and it is a very nice school because Yiayia and Papou have chosen it especially for you. God bless you, my children. Goodnight."

CHAPTER TWO

A New Start

Mateus had already left the house and headed off to his new job by the time the fireball of burning hot Australian sun rose above the horizon. Today was going to be a scorcher, even by Australian standards, as the mercury climbed well into the high forties. Cyprus could similarly sizzle at such high temperatures though he thought it lacked the same burning intensity; it was far hotter in Australia than anywhere else he'd ever been. This morning Mateus was already breaking a sweat because he had signed up for a manual labourer position working with a construction company, which meant long hours outside in the sweltering heat. Although it wasn't his first preference as a steel fabricator, the money was decent, and, most days, Mateus liked that he could finish earlier, take the afternoons off.

Apollo would be starting his first year of high school at Moonee Ponds Central while his younger brother would attend Coburg West Primary School just around the corner from their new home. What troubled Apollo wasn't that he had to speak English: both boys had already learned very good English back in Cyprus and had pretty much mastered the language; no, the problem was that he was starting high school in another country and knew he wouldn't be comfortable at an age where peer relationships were all-important and where all the kids already had their routines and knew each other, while he didn't know a soul. Apollo felt completely out of his comfort zone altogether; so, while his brother jumped around excitedly, eager to meet the new kids at school, Apollo was dreading it.

The family spent the next couple of weeks adjusting to the new ways, customs and cultures of their new country. Mateus had to obtain his new licence, converting it from Cyprus to Victoria, while Mary was dedicated to spending time with her parents, bonding with both of them, and sorting out change of address details, organising the boys' school appointments, uniforms, public transport and school curriculums. It was a hectic time and full-on for her as a mother as they all tried to find their footing and adapt to new routines and a new way of life. Mary also had exceptional English, which benefited her greatly when having to arrange and coordinate so many new moving parts.

Finally, January 25th arrived, and it was time for the boys' first day of school. Apollo arrived at his new school in his new school uniform and with a look of great fear and trepidation—as one would expect of a newcomer. He had always had to wear a school uniform in Cyprus as well; it modelled itself on the British school system, which was in part why Apollo's English was so strong: he'd had to do an hour of language studies every day followed by extensive homework. Apollo walked down the hallway following a bigger kid who was much older and bigger than he and who had been designated to shepherd him and show him around the school grounds. One of the first things Apollo came across was the large sporting oval; he was so excited to see that the school had a soccer oval that for a moment all his fear evaporated and he beamed with pure excitement. Soccer had been Apollo's greatest love back home in Cyprus; Mateus had signed him up to play soccer for the juniors, and, from a young age, Apollo had shown a natural talent; he was small on the field, but he had the athleticism and speed combined with the dribbling skills required to play. He had fast footwork too and was light and quick on his feet to easily manoeuvre the ball and weave in and out and around other players. Apollo thought this was something that he would most surely set out to do at his new school, and he suddenly felt more positive overall about being there.

"I can't wait to play soccer here. I'm definitely going to have fun with that!" he said to no-one in particular but himself. The older kid turned around briefly just then and said, "Huh?" but Apollo couldn't be bothered repeating it; besides, he didn't want to take the risk of embarrassing himself.

He continued to follow the older kid around for a bit before being escorted to his first classroom, which happened to be where his form room teacher and main point of contact, Mr Allcosh, taught. Mr Allcosh would be his history teacher as well as the person he should go to, should he have any concerns or need someone to turn to. Apollo looked around nervously as he nodded his head and greeted some of his peers; there were some bigger, taller boys as well as tall, skinny girls in the classroom, and Apollo took note of how tall Australian kids seemed to be in general, compared to the Greek kids he'd left behind in Cyprus.

"Wow, the Australian girls are pretty," he muttered to himself, and, just then, a couple of girls smiled back at Apollo; he immediately became shy and dropped his head, fearing they'd overheard him. *Damn!* he thought to himself. *This is so not cool, especially not on the first day of school!* Apollo barely managed to return his gaze to the front of the classroom as the teacher began with a formal introduction, and Apollo could feel himself growing horribly self-conscious as his cheeks burned bright red.

Class started, and Mr Allcosh advised his students that they were free to ask as many questions as they desired. "This is a classroom for learning; therefore, there can be no stupid questions in my classroom—because every question is simply another opportunity to learn," Mr Allcosh stated wisely, addressing his new class.

"And I would particularly like to welcome those new students that have just joined us; I can see a few new faces out there, so don't be shy, and, please, everyone try to make them feel welcome just as you would wish to be welcomed." Apollo felt his cheeks burn the same flaming red again as several students turned around just then, acknowledging him as one of the new kids. The bell rang out for lunch just then, and Apollo, feeling relieved, filed out the door behind them, following the cattle of kids as they all headed outside to the school cafeteria.

One of the shorter kids, a freckled, bespectacled boy with mad raven hair came and sat himself down next to Apollo at the empty lunch table.

"Is this seat taken?" the kid genuinely wanted to know.

"Be my guest," Apollo gestured, opening up the sandwich Yiayia had packed for him that morning. He watched as the boy took out a plain, buttered bread roll, then proceeded to bust open a packet of cheese Twisties, which he then sprinkled all over it.

"If you're wondering what this is, we call it a Twistie roll Down

Under. It's basically like putting a bag of chips in your sandwich. Kinda weird, huh? Welcome to Australia, mate—we do everything upside down here."

Apollo nodded, not knowing what to say to the kid, but he himself had already noticed a few things that were different. For instance, the hot and cold taps were back to front, and the light switches on the wall turned on and off in reverse. Even the toilet flushed in an anticlockwise direction, which made Apollo laugh.

"Hey, wanna try one?" the kid asked, holding open the packet of cheese chips. Apollo hesitated, then took a chip.

"Thanks."

"If you're also wondering, this isn't my natural hair colour either—I dyed it this mad raven shade because I got sick of the kids teasing me for having red hair. So you know what? One day I shocked them all and put in some black and blue, and then my parents went all troppo on me instead! You just can't win sometimes, right?"

"Right. Troppo? What's that?" Apollo asked, feeling stupid.

"Oh, just mad—you know, flipping ooouuut. Like parents do."

"Oh, okay, I get it," Apollo said, although the reality was that he didn't get it at all. Good little Greek boys never dared get in trouble with their parents. The Greek Orthodox religion they'd been raised in was strict, and Apollo and Troy had been taught dutifully to respect their parents and elders at all times, so answering back or flipping out wasn't even an option in his world.

Apollo went back to his sandwich, a plain bread and butter sandwich, and he began squeezing the juice of a fresh lemon all over it. Apollo loved putting lemon on anything—and everything—he ate, from breakfast eggs to sandwiches and pasta. The kid, noticing what Apollo was doing, stopped eating his Twistie roll and just stared at him. Feeling self-conscious, Apollo quickly packed the sandwich away again in his lunch box. But the kid wouldn't let him off that easy.

"Hey, what was that? What are you doing—putting lemon on bread?" the kid asked quizzically.

"N-N-nothing," Apollo stammered, not wanting to draw attention to himself. He could feel his face burning up again, and he willed it all to just stop, go away. The kid sensed his embarrassment and backed off.

"No worries, mate—I'll leave ya to it—I don't judge nobody, 'coz I know how that feels," he said, pointing back at his hair.

"Right, no worries," Apollo repeated in his thick European accent; he hoped this kid would just leave him alone. He wasn't sure about the worries part, though, so he though he'd better check. "Did you just say you have worries? Are you okay? What does that mean?" Apollo asked sincerely, feeling puzzled. The kid just chuckled.

"Nah, mate—here in Australia we say 'no worries,' which basically just means no problem, everything's cool. Right, well, nice meeting you, I'll see you around then," the kid said, flicking back his mad raven hair and flashing Apollo a peace sign with his fingers as he left.

By all accounts the rest of Apollo's classes seemed to go well, and, by the end of the day, he could say he had truly enjoyed it. Mr Allcosh's history class on ancient Greece was immediately something he could relate to, it being so much a part of his native culture and heritage. While he enjoyed his history class, Apollo also met his other five teachers in English, Geography, Mathematics, Science and Music—the only teacher he had yet to meet was Mr Burns for Physical Education, but PE only ran on Fridays, so he had a whole week to wait. When Apollo finally returned home Troy was already there to greet him, and they sat down to a Greek snack of Keftethakia, Yiayia's cold Greek meatballs, and to do their homework and talk about their first day at their respective new schools. Troy liked to dip his meatballs in tsatsiki dip, but Apollo didn't like tsatsiki, so he just ate his meatballs plain. Troy got bored pretty quickly, however, in trying to do his homework and dropped his pencil down on the kitchen table emphatically.

"Let's ask Papou if he'll take us to play video games," he said exasperated, packing up his workbook.

"Yeah, that's a good idea," said Apollo, "It's been a long first day, huh?" he remarked, patting his younger brother on the back. Frank was only too happy to walk the boys to the local milk bar, where they could play all their favourite video arcade games: *Frogger, Space Invaders* and *PAC-MAN* were there as well as some new games they'd never seen. The boys couldn't believe their luck with the deluxe array of games they had to choose from. After a couple of hours, they walked home, since the milk bar was only a few hundred metres away; it was so easy and convenient for them all.

"Once you boys get to know your way around, you can do some chores to earn pocket money; then you can go to the milk bar all by yourselves and have fun—but first you have to earn it," Frank said, patting the top of Troy's head.

"Wow, Papou! Thank you! Thank you! Yes! Yes! We want chores!" they both chimed in like dancing monkeys.

Mary had been out shopping with her mother Angela at Coburg Mall all day, and they had even enjoyed some quality mother and daughter time out at the movies. *Labyrinth* had been playing at the cinemas, and they came home to the boys sitting at the table and eating fish and chips for dinner with their Papou.

"Not all that fried Australian junk, Frank! The boys have to eat proper Greek meals too," Yiayia complained. Just then, Mateus came through the front door looking tired and defeated.

"Hi, Levendi mou," Mary greeted her husband, but Mateus was in a sour mood.

"Yeah, hey," was all Mateus could bring himself to say. "Had a rough day—" he muttered with a look that said it all. "Got slapped around with a few racist remarks and slurs amongst some of the work colleagues—Sorry, I'm not really in any kind of mood to talk about it, think I'll just go crash on the bed," he said, heading straight to the fridge and grabbing some liquor. Frank and Angela exchanged a look, and when Mateus was down the hall and out of earshot they gently and softly told their daughter to not let it get to her, that things would be okay.

"It is always tough going in the beginning; it was the same way for me and your mother—it just takes time, love. Be patient."

Yet the boys were excited that, despite their father's bad mood, things had gone well for them; Apollo returned to his plate and squeezed lemon juice all over his fish and chips while Troy talked on and on about his first day and the new friends he'd made. Apollo was sure that Troy found making friends an easier task than he did; for one thing, Apollo was more sensitive and shy whereas Troy seemed more easygoing and unaffected by life. Whatever it was, Apollo prayed it would surely pass and that, in time, he would make new friends the way Troy had. He just needed some time.

CHAPTER THREE

Alora

Over the coming weeks at school, Apollo continued to do well; he'd had a great start to his education and was well on top of his grades and his homework and had even joined the school soccer team. He had started making some new friends, even though he was shy and much more reserved than his younger brother. More than that, though, Apollo had developed something of a new crush: there was a girl in his class, a Greek girl who had quickly caught his eye. Alora Poilitis was a Greek beauty; a petite and pretty, blue-eyed brunette with eyes as blue as the azure Mediterranean sea, and she struck him as the most stunning creature right from the outset. Maybe, it wasn't her looks at all; maybe, it was just her demeanour and easy personality, the way she paid attention to him, smiled and made him feel as though he was real and the only boy in the room. Whatever it was, Alora felt like a drug, and he just wanted more of it. Back home, Apollo had had many girlfriends and childhood crushes; his hazel green eyes, long

Greek eyelashes and boyish smile always got him in trouble with the girls, and this was no exception. At this new school though, Apollo found the Australian girls playful; they liked teasing him and flirting with him even though he didn't know how to take it all. He felt like a fish out of water most of the time because he couldn't understand the lingo or the Aussie jokes they stirred him with, so he just laughed nervously and tried to make the best of it. But Alora soon became his favourite, because he felt he could be himself around her and because she never judged him.

Apollo didn't go unnoticed by Alora either, although she would be the one who would play hard to get with Apollo. He had seen this play out before between his mother and father, too, so by thirteen, Apollo had a firm grip on the dance between the sexes, the rules of the game. Alora would flutter her eyelids at Apollo, flash a big flirty smile in his direction and seem interested; when he'd finally muster enough courage to go over and talk to her, she would turn demure, shy. It was the blossoming of young love, and Apollo loved all of it.

"Bye, Yiayia! I gotta get to school!" Apollo sang out, racing through the kitchen and grabbing his lunch before bolting out the door.

"Well, it's so refreshing to see such enthusiasm in that boy for his new school. He really loves learning! My beautiful little Greek boy is going to be one smart man one of these days," Yiayia said proudly.

"Oh, that's not why he's in such a hurry, Mama; there's a girl on the scene! Troy said he has seen Apollo talking to a pretty brunette by the bus stop," Mary teased, and raised an eyebrow playfully at her mother.

"There's nothing healthier for a young man than the attentions of a pretty girl ... Does their confidence wonders," Yiayia remarked honestly. "Speaking of which, I see that hardworking husband of yours looking pretty tired lately. Why don't you get yourself all prettied up and have a night out on the town? You both need some time together, and you've had very little of that lately. Papou and I will take care of the boys; now go on, go and get your hair done before I change my mind," Yiayia winked and went back to her cleaning in the kitchen. It didn't take much to convince Mary to go spend money on herself; she loved nothing more than buying nice clothes and getting all dolled up, and she had expensive tastes, too. She decided she would go on Yiayia's advice and make an appointment to get her hair and nails done; this would definitely get her husband's attention, she thought.

Apollo raced towards the bus stop, and, sure enough, there was Alora standing by a street sign, school bag slung over one shoulder talking with a group of girls. They all looked the same in a cluster of blue uniforms, but it was Alora's slender, petite figure and radiant blue eyes that immediately jumped out at him. He could feel himself growing very nervous as he passed them by; not knowing what to do and feeling stupidly shy, Apollo looked back at Alora and shyly mouthed a small 'Hi' in her direction. Alora beamed back at him, and the cackle of girls surrounding her all noticed the exchange.

"Oooh, so who's that, Alora? Is that your new loverboy? He's new, isn't he?" her friend Tracy cooed, teasingly. Tracy was the tallest girl, blonde and skinny, with boys on the brain disease.

"Oh, he's in my English class—his name is Apollo and he's just moved to Australia from Cyprus," chubby Amanda chimed in. "He is a really good reader, too; Mrs Wilcox calls on him to read all the time, and he speaks perfect English."

By now Apollo had made his way onto the bus, but he couldn't take the back seat because that was where all the cool kids sat, so, instead, he slipped into a seat halfway down the aisle and buried his head in his constant companion, *The Count of Monte Cristo*. The girls boarded the bus then, and as they walked by his seat Tracy made an 'oooh oooh' teasing sound, which made Apollo blush.

By now, he had sensed some of the boys wanting to give him a hard time, and, sure enough, after he climbed off the bus, one of the boys came up behind Apollo, giving him a hard shove in the back. Gavin Croosy was a bigger boy who was in Apollo's year; he was a tall lanky kid with a sharp tongue, an aggressive attitude and snapped like a short fuse, and he had a reputation for being the class bully.

"Hey, ya fucking wog. Think the girls like you now, huh? Fucking coming here," Croosy said, pushing him again. Apollo was no fighter; far from it. He was academic and good at soccer, but his short frame and structure made him an easy target. Foolishly and perhaps naively, Apollo decided to fire back, not considering the repercussions and secretly wondering what the word wog meant.

"Fuck you," he retorted angrily, but the look in Gavin Croosy's eyes told him he was going to come back at Apollo every chance he got. Croosy spat at the gravel by the outdoor basketball court and glared at him.

"What did ya just say, cunt?" Gavin slurred, then before Apollo knew it, he came quickly at him, grabbing him by the scruff of his shirt just as two of Gavin's other friends, Simon Libb, and Cale Moss appeared from around the corner. By now, all the kids including Alora had gone into their respective classrooms and Apollo tensed up, sensing what he had predicted was about to turn into open slather as the only kid left on the playground.

"Hit the wog! Hit him, the lippy cunt," Simon and Cale shouted from a short distance away, encouraging Gavin to take the first shot at Apollo. Apollo saw Gavin's fist clench in response to the dare, and, not knowing what to do, he did what he knew he could do best: run. Apollo could run rings around pretty much any kid; despite his small frame, he was gifted with great running ability and fast reflexes, so he could easily outrun most of the kids; the soccer field and athletic track were indeed his truest friends. His father also often said that, with his agility, Apollo would make a fine lightweight boxer; but Apollo had zero fighting ability in him. Apollo knew he would only ever be a lover, not a fighter. But, for right now, his only thought was to run in order to save himself, so he thought of his friend Massimo, and then and he ran like the wind.

This was to mark the beginning of a long road ahead of bullying. For days on end afterwards, the boys began to use the back of Apollo's head in class as constant target practice, launching spit balls, paper flips, whatever they could get their hands on, and aiming it in his general direction.

Apollo's short stature didn't help matters, and they singled him out, forcing him to endure the constant harassment of name-calling and mean words, belittling him whenever the teachers weren't around or within earshot.

"Hey there, ya midget, ya short arse, ya little wog cunt ... Why won't you talk to us? What're ya afraid of?" Apollo cringed quietly in his seat and wished he could just disappear; he wasn't one for wanting to go to the teachers because he didn't want to be labelled weak, or a tattletale—so he tried to tough it out the best he could and avoided the boys on the playground because life was just easier that way. Instead, Apollo decided to go to the school library at lunch hour, because he knew the boys wouldn't follow him there. Books had always been Apollo's refuge, and here they were, saving him again. He walked through the large, double glass doors, and the friendly librarian, Mrs Mitcham, smiled at him.

"I think you're one of the new students; here, let me get you a new library card. If you like books as much as I do, then you're going to need this," she said smiling and handing him a library card. Apollo took an instant liking to Mrs Mitcham and thought she looked funky in a pair of square, pink-rimmed glasses.

"Thank you—can you tell me where I can find the dictionaries?" Apollo asked politely.

"Why yes, they are just over here, let me show you, dear," Mrs Mitcham said and came out from behind the check-in desk. She walked Apollo down past aisles of books, and he followed her, inhaling the leathery, papery scent of shelves and shelves of books. He had never seen so many books in his life.

"Here. Use this one—it's the latest Merriam-Webster dictionary. I think you'll find what you need in there," Mrs Mitcham smiled then pranced away back to her post at the front desk.

Apollo opened the large volume; it was too heavy in his hands, so he decided to sit down in the cubicle closest to him. He began scanning the pages with his index finger, going through the letters of the alphabet and turning the pages carefully so as not to damage them. His brain was doing an internal dance between the Greek alphabet and the English alphabet as he silently mouthed Alpha, Beta, Gamma, Delta, Epsilon to himself so that no-one would hear him. He had to try to look less Greek now; he had to stand out less. To him, it was a matter of life and death.

Finally, he got to the letter W. *Wog, wog, wog, wog,* he said to himself. *Where was it? What did it mean?* He couldn't find any definition of it anywhere. Frustrated, he decided to return to the check-in desk and Mrs Mitcham.

"Umm, hello," Apollo muttered in almost a half-whisper.

"Hello again there, young man—did you find what you were looking for?"

"Umm, well actually no—not really," Apollo replied, solemnly shaking his head.

"Well, can I help at all? Maybe I can find what you're looking for," Mrs Mitcham said helpfully. Apollo looked up at this woman; he had to figure out if he thought she was nice or not. What if he told her? Would she be kind, or would she just laugh at him? He couldn't bring himself to face any more ridicule, yet he tried to remind himself that, on first impressions, she had seemed like a kind lady, so maybe …

"I'm looking to find out what the word 'Wog' means," Apollo ventured nervously. Mrs Mitcham looked at Apollo and slowly put down the book she had been holding.

"Okaaay," Mrs Mitcham replied carefully. Now she was looking seriously over the tops of the rims of her glasses down at the boy. "Do I sense that we have a little problem going on here?" she asked softly.

"Er … never mind," Apollo winced, backing away from the desk. The last thing he needed right now was for word to get out amongst the teaching staff that he was being bullied. He was the new kid at school, and he needed to stay cool and fly under the radar for a while, and then hopefully, he would make some new friends—because he certainly wasn't going to gain any popularity by going this way and involving any of the teachers. Apollo continued backing away from the desk and then without another word he turned and exited through the large glass doors. He felt alone having no-one to talk to, yet he couldn't explain any of it yet, anyway; he just hoped it would all die down and somehow magically go away.

When the bell rang at 3:30pm, Apollo gathered his things and headed for the athletics field; while he didn't particularly enjoy the PE class every Friday, he couldn't wait to get to the soccer and athletics track. Back in Cyprus, his school had been centred on academics, with some sports activities being offered; but, here at his new school, Apollo couldn't believe the range of different subjects available to him, including art, music and science. Strangely enough, there were never any arts or music classes taught in Cyprus; despite a wonderful Cyprian heritage of theatre, art, dance and music, these subjects were barely touched on, because the focus was placed purely on academic achievement, where even the very youngest children were expected to do hours of homework each night in language and mathematics. There were a few small institutes or odeons, as they were called, that focused on the arts, but there were certainly no full-time schools that provided teaching in music—and with only one official tertiary institution, The University of Cyprus, offering courses in business studies or information technology of some kind, the opportunities open to most Cypriots were pretty limited, with many leaving to attend schools in London instead.

Apollo changed into his running shorts and then he emerged from the boys' locker rooms so fast he almost collided headlong into Alora, who was on her way to an after-school music program.

"Sorry, I didn't see you coming," Apollo said nervously, hoping his voice wouldn't wobble.

"Oh, that's okay. I wasn't looking where I was going either,"

Alora replied sweetly. Her voice was as soft as butter, and Apollo immediately felt himself melting into her; it was the first time he'd heard her soft, sweet melody.

"You always look so serious," Alora said, again sweetly, trying to make conversation.

"Oh—sorry," Apollo stammered, not knowing what to say. Apology was forever his default line because he quite simply could never think of anything to say.

"Oh no, that wasn't a criticism—now I'm sorry, too!" Alora stated apologetically, which made them both laugh. This was becoming a nice icebreaker, Apollo thought to himself. He stood there admiring her for a moment longer, thinking how Greek and perfect she was, before thinking he should move on or he would be late.

"Well, I've got to get to athletics practice," Apollo said, feeling clumsy and bashful.

"Okay, no worries. I'll see you soon," Alora smiled and drifted away.

There were those words again, 'no worries'. Apollo liked the way that sounded, how she sounded—because deep down he knew he was a worrier, and the truth of it was that he probably worried just a little bit too much—about everything. But hadn't she just said that she'd 'see him soon'? The mere thought of this sent Apollo into the clouds; he was floating on air as he walked away. *She wants to see me*, he thought. *Wow. And she wants to see me soon. Does that mean she likes him? Double wow.* Apollo walked onto the field grinning like a frigging idiot; he felt higher than a kite and just couldn't believe his luck. The day had started off such a nightmare with Gavin Croosy after him—and now here he was on cloud nine with Alora. How quickly things could turn on a dime, he realised. One minute he was living an ordinary childhood in Cyprus, and now, here he was, halfway around the world and living in a new country, and a beautiful Greek girl was taking notice of him. Life was just full of surprises.

Thoughts of Alora propelled Apollo to run even harder at athletics practice that day; it also fuelled the hatred and jealousy the other boys were developing for him.

At some level, Apollo knew that this bullying was all part of the fact that he outshone them all; not only was he excelling in mathematics and English (despite English being his second language), now he was literally running rings around these boys on the athletics track—their home turf—and he could feel the resentment climbing as he sprinted past a sea of red-hot faces. It's always hard enough to be the new kid in town; but, when the new kid starts to look too good, it always ends up causing problems. Apollo wished he could just close his eyes and teleport himself back to Cyprus, back to his bedroom and his school and his life and his good friend, Massimo.

"Υεια—yassou, hello boys, how're you going, how's school going?" Papou asked later that afternoon, taking to his favourite reclining chair in the family room. Yiayia detested the piece of furniture, saying it 'wrecked the decor of the room' because it looked so modern and out of place next to her Greek furniture. Troy was sprawled out on the mustard and brown '80s rug in front of the television set, working his portable game of *Donkey Kong*, while Apollo had curled up like a cat on the beige, neoclassical '80s-style sofa, exhausted from a full afternoon of athletics. The '70s wallpaper overhead was a funky gold colour covered in a Greek key dental overlay pattern, which Apollo thought really did look like oversized teeth, and the cold marble flooring and Greek urns, amphoras, leant an Aegean Mediterranean vibe to the home. Two klismos-style chairs with scroll arms reminiscent of small thrones sat facing one another and completed the look.

Papou rested a cold beer down on the small cadiz side table next to the recliner and made a grunting sound as he sat down. His knees were bothering him in old age, and he rubbed furiously at them in an effort to relieve his pain. Since neither of the boys answered him about his day, Papou reached for the remote control and began flipping channels at random. Not long after, Mateus came through the door covered in dirt, his face sour. Troy sprang to his feet to greet his father.

"No, no, get off me! I have to go take a shower. Can't you see I'm dirty?" Mateus said, trying to get his son off him. But Troy clung to his father's jacket like a monkey; he had barely seen his father of late, and his absence at the family dinner table had been palpable. Mary walked in the room just then, looking stunning in a tight-fitting red dress, its curves accentuating every aspect of her body like a road map. Mateus did a double take.

"Well, where have you been, all dressed up like that?" he muttered, more than a hint of jealousy escaping his lips. Mary shot him an angry look.

"I have been to the hair salon, if that's what you mean," she spat back at him, "Making an effort to look nice for you on our date tonight, remember?"

Mateus rolled his eyes. He was tired and dirty and just needed a shower. The last thing he needed was a night out.

"Okay, okay—I get it, I get it—it's all for me, there's nothing in it for you—" he shot back sarcastically.

"Ah, fungula malaka!—I was just trying to do something nice for us, Mateus, that was all," Mary bit back, feeling defeated.

"Hey, watch your language around the children! This is my house after all, Mary!" Papou barked at his daughter. Mateus and Mary looked at each other; they both realised Papou had spoken, and therefore, a silent truce was in order. Mateus, wanting to de-escalate matters, went to the fridge and grabbed himself a beer and took a big swig.

"Where are we going anyway?" he asked, in an attempt to lighten the mood.

"What's fungoooooola?" little Troy chimed in. Mary rolled her eyes. Great, Mateus thought. Just great. He shot Mary a death look and walked off down the hall to the bathroom. Mary could see Mateus was angry and not happy with his job; he had become snippy, aggressive, and short with her ever since they'd arrived in Australia, and in her mind, the tension between them was just getting worse. So much for the nice evening out, Mary thought bitterly to herself. She sat down on the edge of Papou's recliner, and he wrapped an arm around his daughter.

"I understand what you were trying to do, and you do look lovely, my beautiful princess, koukla mou—and you will always be my girl, but go easy on that husband of yours. He is under a lot of pressure at the moment, being the man of the house and all—"

"Ugh—you men are all the same! You always just stick together!" Mary cried and stormed out of the room, slamming the door. Apollo looked up from the sofa; he wished he could talk to his parents, but ever since they had arrived in Australia things had been different, and no-one seemed to have any time for anyone anymore. Not that he was in the mood for any type of discussion, anyway; it just seemed as if everyone was preoccupied with themselves and their own problems, and he was missing the closeness they'd shared as a family unit back in Cyprus. Yes, the house had felt cramped and been too small for them at times, but at least they had always been together; they had always had each other. Now he couldn't even tell who these people were anymore, so he just lay there on the sofa looking up at the wall, noticing the flecks of paint falling away, the cracks that were appearing under the once pretty gold wallpaper.

CHAPTER FOUR

A Divided Land

C yprus has been divided since 1974 when Turkish troops invaded and occupied the northern third of the island in response to a coup sponsored by the military junta, then ruling Greece. Ankara's intervention followed a decade of intercommunal tension and violence between the Greek majority and the Turkish minority and the deployment of UN peacekeepers. The division saw some 200,000 people forced from their homes. Nicosia, the capital city of Cyprus, is the only capital in the world that remains divided between two nations. The city is divided by 'The Green Line,' which is also known as the UN buffer zone. Almost forty-four years later, Cyprus remains cut in two and a barrier of barbed wire and military posts makes the capital Nicosia the world's last divided city. However, the inhabitants on both sides have managed to coexist peacefully.

Apollo couldn't remember much about the tensions that existed in Cyprus at the time; he was too young to experience any of it, and his parents had worked hard to shelter the boys from the goings-on in the outside world. To him, Cyprus' ruins had always been in plain sight; one could tour the archaeological sites of the ancient Kourion situated on a coastal bluff, or visit the Tomb of the Kings. But now things were different, and Apollo wasn't sure if it was because he was getting older and understanding more, or whether things just weren't being hidden as much as they had been, and now everything was just in plain sight.

Mary and Mateus had ventured out for the evening, and the boys enjoyed Yiayia's eggplant moussaka for dinner, followed by a game of Tavli. Afterwards, Papou sipped on a glass of ouzo while Yiayia answered many questions about her childhood.

"So, when you came to Australia, you had nothing?" Apollo asked, astounded.

"You mean, you didn't even have your parents, like we do?" little Troy asked, incredulous. If his eyes had grown any wider, Apollo thought, they would have popped.

"No my child, we had nothing … we had only a few minutes to gather our possessions, you see; the Turkish military were moving in, entrenching its position in response to a coup that had been aimed at uniting the island with Greece. When that didn't work, most Cypriots were robbed of their past overnight, turning them into refugees. It was awful, I tell you! I remember the only thing my mother managed to take were her threads and embroideries—we had to leave photo albums, everything we owned, behind. All I have now are my memories—and they will never take that!" Yiayia cried emphatically. She paused for a moment and looked over longingly at the mantelpiece, which held many framed photos of her and Papou's Greek Cypriot relatives.

"Did you ever want to go back?" Apollo asked. He had been

thinking a lot about home lately, especially after being bullied at school, and he thought about how much easier things had been for him at his old school, how he had been so easily accepted compared to now, because there he was one of them, he belonged there.

"Oh, for years, I dreamed of returning to my homeland, but you don't understand: it just was not possible. There was one time, and one time only, when my mother did go back and see it, and it was after the war …

"And?"

"Her family had lived on the island since 1860, mind you—yet they would not let her in; instead, they told her she was now a refugee and she no longer had any rights to her property or her land; it was the greatest sin," Yiayia explained, crossing her chest with her hand in prayer.

Apollo could see Papou's face becoming enraged; Yiayia said he often got this way whenever they talked about the invasion of '74, so even as Yiayia spoke and Apollo listened, his eyes never left Frank.

"You must understand, Apollo," Yiayia continued, "the Cypriots have always been very attached to their land, so what happened to them was an abomination to their peaceful way of life. Even now I can still recall the scent of the lemon trees, the smell of the sea, the dappled light and the way it filtered through the citrus orchards of Lapithos, where my ancestors were born …

Apollo and Troy were still young, young enough not to understand so many things, but in that moment when Yiayia was speaking what they could fully understand was the sadness in her heart, all the things she had lost, Apollo couldn't hold back the tears any longer.

"I am so sorry for you, Yiayia," he cried, and sobbed into the shoulder of her dress. He didn't know why he was crying exactly, but his crying made Troy sad too, and soon he too began to cry and then they were all crying and Papou was wiping his eyes with his sleeve and telling them to all stop because he needed another ouzo.

When it was time for bed, Yiayia tucked them in and told them another story from her childhood; there were endless stories of Cyprus, which the boys loved to listen to because it made them feel more at home somehow. Apollo closed his eyes and imagined himself back in his old bedroom, looking out through the makeshift curtain at the starry night sky, a balmy breeze dancing through the curtain and lulling him off to sleep. He could picture the neighbour's cat with her emerald eyes and jet black fur juxtaposed against the whitewashed stone walls, and the way she swung her tail back and forth temperamentally under a full moon. There would always be moments like this, Apollo thought, where he would drift between the past and the future and find himself caught somewhere in-between that left him feeling lost and alone.

Troy was snoring contentedly and Apollo had just closed his eyes again when he was awakened by a disturbance coming from down the hall. He recognised it as his mother's voice as it climbed an octave and held that bitter, scratchy tone he knew all too well whenever she fought with their father. Mateus was usually the first to back down because when he and his mother argued it was she who usually won; she could be willful and stubborn and downright childish sometimes. Apollo noted that, if she ever thought she was losing an argument, she would turn it to tears. This made their father feel guilty to the point where he would back down and acquiesce to whatever it was she wanted. She was used to getting her own way, and it could turn to hellfire and brimstone if anyone challenged her.

"You just don't get it—" Apollo could hear his father say in a raised voice. "You come prancing in here in all that silly getup, looking all slutty, and yet all day, I've been breaking my back out there in that fucking hot sun, labouring away, while you waste all our goddamn money on fucking hair and nails and jewellery for yourself! Can't you see how selfish you're being?"

"I was just trying to make myself beautiful for you, Mateus, but as usual, you don't appreciate anything that I do! And I was only listening to Mama's advice: she was the one who suggested it!"

"Well, she didn't suggest that you throw yourself at the fucking waiter!"

"Oh, grow up, Mateus. Are you serious? He was just a little Italian boy working in the Lygon Street fete! You have to be joking now …"

"I give up, Mary; I'm sick of going around and around like this—I'm going to bed because one of us has to fucking work tomorrow!"

"Raising children is work too: it's a full-time job, and I don't even get paid!"

"Oh, come on, Mary! Your mother does everything for them—I've never seen you lift a finger! Yiayia cooks, she cleans, she even puts the kids to bed …"

"Fuck you, Mateus! Fungoola malaka!"

"Fungoola malaka to you, too!"

Door slams. Picture falls off the wall. Apollo just lay there and listened quietly to the sounds of his parents fighting, doors slamming, things creaking in the night, and he wondered how many more cracks it just made in the wall.

Troy awoke to the sounds of slamming and yelling too. "Is Mama and Papa fighting again?" he asked, rubbing his eyes.

"It's okay, Troy," Apollo said, trying to comfort his little brother. "Just go back to sleep. It's stopped now."

***

The next day started in the same way as all the others; Apollo would try to avoid being seen by Gavin, Simon, and Cale as they were now making a habit of targeting him by the side gate, where his mother now dropped him off. He no longer took the bus because Mary had found part-time work in a security company and could drop Apollo off on her way to work. Apollo rode quietly next to his mother in the passenger seat; he wanted so badly to tell her what had been happening to him at school, but something always stopped him. He knew both his parents had been under a lot of stress and were fighting more and more, and he didn't want to be any more of a burden. He also didn't want to come off as wimpy or weak. Oftentimes, his mother would say, "Apollo, you are a big boy now, and you have to toughen up," but she never offered anything more than this, so Apollo knew that if he went to her, he would never get much in the way of sympathy. His mother had proven herself to be a very tough woman who knew how to use her beauty and her wiles to get what she wanted, and she didn't have much time for sensitivity or feelings because this, to her, was a sign of weakness. But now it had become apparent that Gavin, Simon and Cale's favourite pastime was to wait by the gate ready to taunt Apollo. It was by now a morning ritual and a game every day, Monday through Friday, so Apollo had started to walk back the opposite direction from where he was dropped off, just to avoid the confrontation. This of course meant he was now almost always a few minutes late to class as he waited by a tree, deliberately stalling his arrival in order to avoid the boys, and this got him in trouble with Mr Allcosh.

"Apollo, we have to have words about your tardiness. I have told you before that you must be in class, ready to start at exactly nine o'clock, no later. It is now 9:05am. If this keeps happening, I will have no choice but to give you detention."

Apollo cringed. Initially, he had liked Mr Allcosh and thought he was pretty cool because he taught history (which happened to be Apollo's favourite subject), but lately Apollo had realised that Mr Allcosh could be an insensitive dickhead, a smart alec and a know-it-all who was cold and distant with his students and showed no compassion at all. When Jane Worthington hadn't come to class for a week, Mr Allcosh had given her a giant red 'F' on her report; her parents came to the school to explain that their daughter had broken her arm in a gymnastics competition, and Mr Allcosh had coldly dismissed their excuse with the argument that she'd still had one good arm to write with. Apollo knew he just couldn't like Mr Allcosh after that, no matter how many A's he gave him on his history assignments.

By midyear, things were progressively getting worse and Apollo began to dread going to school altogether. Some days the boys managed to work out Apollo's tactics for avoiding them, and they would go off in three separate locations in hopes of cutting him off or blocking his entrance to the school grounds. Some days Apollo was able to get away from them; one time he outsmarted them all by arriving early and hiding out behind the school shed. That day, he'd watched the boys as they paced back and forth by the school gate getting drenched in the rain, and Apollo had to laugh, seeing Gavin Croosy fist pump the sky out of sheer frustration with the fact that Apollo hadn't shown up. By the the end of the year, the bullying had gotten so intense that several other boys were privy to it and they joined in, and then, the attacks became more random. Yet no-one would speak up for Apollo, and certainly not Apollo himself, for fear of retribution.

Yet ironically, at the same time, Apollo was also attracting constant female attention, with the girls in his year taking a real liking to him. A few of them were even developing crushes, which completely surprised and floored Apollo. They saw him as the gentle, sensitive type, far from big gronks like Gavin and his mates. Apollo would walk down the school corridors to girls leaning up against their lockers, smiling at him as he passed by.

"That's Apollo. He is such a little cutie," he heard one girl say as headed for his locker. Even Alora's friend, Tracy was now taking a shine to him.

"Hey, sweet thing," Tracy crooned at him when she saw him in the cafeteria at lunchtime. Apollo knew that Tracy oozed a confidence he'd never had, and he envied her smoothness, and the ease with which she could start a conversation with anybody. All the teachers liked Tracy too because she demonstrated a maturity beyond her years. But Alora didn't like Tracy's advances one bit, and Apollo sensed that she was uncomfortable with them; yet he knew Alora could never be as forward, pushy and brazen as Tracy, which only made him like Alora more.

"Why don't you come over here and sit with us at our lunch table?" Tracy sleazed, and Apollo caught sight of Alora in the background quietly rolling her eyes in disgust. He had to suppress his laughter; it felt as if Alora and he could almost read each other's minds most of the time. He winked at her when Tracy wasn't looking because he wanted Alora to know he understood and was nobody's fool; he was in on Tracy's act. But it touched Apollo to know that Alora cared; clearly she cared, seeing as how Apollo knew they had this unspeakable connection, and right then he wished everyone else would just disappear so he could be alone with Alora.

But Apollo's popularity with the girls did him no favours with Gavin, Simon and Cale.

"Oh, you big boy, Apollo. You think you're so hot now," they berated him constantly. They always picked their moments to bully Apollo when there was no-one else around, and Apollo knew this too.

"What ya gonna do if we just come over there right now and flip your lunch tray, huh? You gonna call your mama, little boy?" Apollo looked around in vain to see if any of the lunch duty monitors were witnessing their taunts, but Gavin was strategic and always waited until the cafeteria staff started cleaning up because that meant they would be too busy taking trays out the back and clearing tables to notice.

"Leave me alone, Croosy, I've done nothing to you," Apollo said, trying to fight back; but it didn't seem to matter how often he fought back—and Apollo fought back as often as he could—because he always found himself coming off second best no matter how hard he tried. The sad truth of the matter was that Apollo was simply no match for the bigger boys, and he was always outnumbered and he knew it. And the more he got teased, the worse it became.

Three weeks passed and Apollo could feel his self-confidence waning; now, sadly, a few girls had taken note of the teasing, and they'd caught on to the bullying, too. The next thing Apollo knew, Tracy had joined in and started degrading Apollo as well; even the girls who crushed on Apollo were now bullying him, and they were all laughing as though this was much more fun than flirting with him. As he stood in line at the cafeteria, Gavin and his musketeers would walk by and deliberately bump into Apollo, sending the orange juice on his tray flying. Some days he managed to get away from them; other days he skipped lunch, preferring the quiet sanctuary of the library to their constant taunts. Only Alora seemed to understand, he thought; he would look at her across the cafeteria and see her eyes filled with sentiments of unspoken sympathy.

"They're just insanely jealous of you," Alora said one day, whispering into his ear as she passed by his desk.

"What for?" Apollo whispered back, looking completely baffled.

"Well, for one thing you are excelling in all your school work—and I secretly know that Gavin, Simon and Cale are all completely flunking out in English, history, and maths," Alora smirked.

It was true, Apollo thought; jealousy loomed large over the fact he was academic and gifted from a sports perspective, and certainly he hadn't made things any easier for himself by crushing them all on the athletics field, either.

"They just won't leave me alone," Apollo said, with real sadness in his eyes. He wished he could just hug Alora right then and there; she was such a caring soul and he felt their connection deepening every time he got close to her.

"Don't worry, Apollo; we'll figure this out in time," Alora winked and quickly skitted over to sit at her desk. Apollo felt a warm feeling envelop him then; it was like a warm glow that radiated from the inside out. He truly liked this girl, and he began to sense that she truly liked him, too.

When Apollo got home from school that afternoon his school bag was heavy and laden with books, but his heart felt even heavier. His self-confidence had taken such a big hit that his self-esteem was down in the dumps, but he felt he couldn't burden his mother or grandparents with any of it. To make matters worse, as soon as Apollo stepped in the door he could hear his parents at each other's throats again.

"Why are you lying around being such a fat, lazy asshole—why aren't you out working?" Mary screamed at Mateus, who was lying on the sofa drunk as a skunk.

"I can take the fucking afternoon off if I feel like it!" Mateus slurred between words. That's why I start work before dawn. Leave me the fuck alone, bitch."

"Don't you dare call me that," Mary screamed at him, and her bloodcurdling ripple sent shock waves through the house. She lunged at Mateus then, her freshly painted nails digging into the base of his neck. Mateus scrambled off the couch then, chasing Mary into the kitchen; he grabbed her by her hair and slapped her face with his dirty bare hands. Angela came in the kitchen and screamed at the sight of blood on her kitchen floor and immediately called the police. In fewer than three minutes, the boys in blue were rapping on the door of Angela and Frank's suburban home, and Mateus stumbled outside, escorted outside by the police sergeant for questioning.

Mary clung to her mother Yiayia, and she kept apologising in-between sobs for the scene they had caused in front of the family; meanwhile, Papou had arrived home in the middle of all the commotion looking more than a little dazed and confused.

The boys retreated to their rooms sensing they needed to lie low, and all the while, Apollo heard his father screaming obscenities through the door, yelling at their mother.

"You fucking bitch! This is what you wanted all along! You've ruined everything, you hear me? You've ruined everything."

Troy and Apollo looked at each other across their beds, their faces stricken with worry. Troy began to cry and buried his face in his pillow. With his home life now not in a happy or healthy state, Apollo didn't know where he could turn to. He just felt naked and so very alone. Yet still there was a little voice inside and it spoke to him, telling him that he would just have to go it alone right now; he had to deal with things and live his predicament because, right now, there was just no other way, and, because sometimes when you feel buried so deep, it's impossible to see out from under the ruins.

CHAPTER FIVE

Broken

A pollo was trying to fathom how his life had suddenly turned for the worse. He couldn't comprehend what had happened between his father and mother, and he couldn't make sense of anything; in fact, everything seemed to be falling apart right before his very eyes.

After being aggressive and violent with Mary, Mateus had suddenly left; his job was not going the way he had hoped and planned, and now it was looking as if divorce was on the cards, too. Frank and Angela had struggled with calling the police; they hadn't wanted to cause the couple any more trouble, but Mateus had been so drunk and out of control that Angela felt she'd had no choice.

"Let him go," was all Mary said. "He does nothing for me—nothing at all. You see the way he treats me? He's always screaming at me whenever the boys are at school, or in bed … it's been happening for months now! And he never spends any time with the boys anymore;

he's been distancing himself from us for a while—and he resents the fact that I pushed him to move out here to Australia because he never really wanted to come; he wanted to stay in Cyprus with his brother's family. In fact, if he hadn't lost his job as a steel fabricator, we'd probably still be stuck there. So good riddance to him—I don't need him no more; I can get any man I want!"

Yiayia shook her head; until now, she hadn't realised the full extent of it, or how bad it had gotten between them, and suddenly, she felt as though she were stuck between a rock and a hard place because she loved her daughter, but she loved her son-in-law too. Yet she realised her loyalties ultimately lay with her daughter, so she kept quiet and said nothing.

Troy overheard his mother's hard words and came running to her, crying. Apollo followed close behind.

"Mama! Mama! No! No! Make Daddy come back!" Troy wailed into her dress.

"No, Troy, not now; I cannot deal with this," Mary said, acting cold and distant and pushing Troy off her. She looked at Apollo; she knew as the older child he understood much more than his younger brother.

"But why, Mum? Why?" was all Apollo could muster as his eyes welled with tears.

Troy was much the same. "Yeah, Mum—what about Dad?" he pleaded, his little voice desperate and quavering. But Troy was just too little to understand the problems that surrounded his parents.

"Stop this nonsense, Apollo! You don't understand anything! Don't you start in on me! Can't you see that this is the last thing I need right now? Now both of you go to your room—and don't come out until I say you can!" Mary barked.

Apollo did not need to be told twice. He grabbed his

brother's hand and led him back to their bedroom, with Troy sobbing uncontrollably. Yiayia told them she would come to see them soon enough. Mary glared at her mother.

"Stop playing favourites in this house! And stop trying to make me look like I'm the bad one around here! You're always interfering!" Mary snapped at her mother across the kitchen counter. Yiayia, taken aback by her daughter's unleashed venom, froze on the spot; the sadness in her eyes said it all and she just stood there as an elderly woman, shaking her head.

"Mary, I wasn't doing that at all; I was just trying to comfort them—"

But Mary was in the most belligerent mood and wouldn't hear another word from Yiayia, so instead, she spun on her heels and stormed out of the house, slamming the door behind her.

Apollo was horrified with it all; as a soon to be fourteen-year-old he felt crushed and so alone. The teenage years frightened him, and he lay there quietly on his bed, listening to his brother's sobs echoed in the light pitter-patter of rain upon their window. He had caught wind of his parents troubles a while back, but clearly he had been too absorbed in his own troubles to digest it.

Yiayia came in to comfort her two grandchildren; it broke her to see them so unhappy and she eased herself down gently on the edge of the bed and cuddled them until their tears stopped.

"Your mother and father are going through a difficult time right now, so we have to be patient. Just remember that Yiayia and Papou are always here for you, and we love you both very much. Now who wants some of my special avyolemoni egg and rice soup? It's very comforting."

But Apollo wasn't hungry, and Troy just buried his head further into his pillow.

"Okay, I'll take that as a 'no' for now; maybe you boys would like a special story with Yiayia instead. Let me tuck into bed with you," she said, climbing under the covers. Both boys snuggled into Yiayia's armpits as she began her story.

"We still have land there, you know—land that was stolen by the Turks. I grew up in a town called Famagusta, a walled city on the north-east coastline, about an hour from the capital, Nicosia, in the central region, and not far from the Güsleren barracks, a military base set up after the coup. I remember being so scared—just like you boys are now—and I scrambled to get my most prized posessions, like my rings, some jewellery, this lamp here ... and a few portrait paintings—it was all such a blur, because everything happened so fast and we had no time to react, no time at all. After the Turkish army invaded us—I think it was called Operation Atilla, or something like that—it resulted in a coup; then the army controlled Varosha until the UN brokered a ceasefire, which marked the end of the invasion. After that they fenced off Famagusta completely, refusing any visitors or residents from ever returning. Today it sits abandoned, a ghost town, and there is nothing left of the place, nothing there at all, except for the ghosts of our memories."

"You mean, you could never ever go home again?" Troy asked his grandmother tearfully.

"No my precious moleki mou; it used to be a once beautiful resort town for the rich and famous, but after it was subjected to shelling it turned to wreck and ruin. But oh, it used to be such a picture postcard! It had over three hundred churches that rang out daily across the land ... I do so miss the sound of the bells ..." Yiayia said wistfully.

"... and so where did you go then?" Apollo asked, his curiosity now piqued.

"Well, your grandfather and I had to make new lives for ourselves here, so you must realise that life is sometimes tough like this; you will always face hard times in your life because life is not supposed to be all fun and games: life is supposed to be suffering. If life was always happy, then how would we ever be able to know the good times from the bad?"

"I don't think life can get much worse for me than it is now, Yiayia," Apollo hinted quietly under his breath.

"Nothing lasts forever, my child; bad times will always come—but the good news is that bad times will always go away, too. I have always liked the saying 'this too shall pass,' because, if you just wait a little while and let the moment pass, the sun always rises again. Now: are you sure you don't want some of my yummy soup?"

But Troy was now rubbing his eyes and Yiayia noticed it was well past the boys' bedtime, so she tucked them both in and kissed their foreheads, wishing them goodnight. She made sure to leave the soft night light on for them too in case they needed her through the night.

***

Mary did not come home that night, and, when the boys woke, they were asking all sorts of questions, but Yiayia busied them to eat up their breakfast, announcing that she would be taking them both to school instead. Apollo climbed out of the car dragging his feet; it felt as though his troubles at home and at school were now colliding, and he felt as though soon he was going to be taken out by a giant tsunami. He had heard nothing from his father, only whisperings between his mother and grandmother that Mateus had taken up with a new Australian woman, Olivia Bridges, news which enraged his mother no end.

One afternoon, Mary stormed in the door carrying a letter in her hand; she slammed it down on the table so hard it caused one of the wine goblets to wobble and shatter. Papou looked up from his newspaper with a disapproving frown, and Yiayia quickly got up from the table to clean up the mess.

"The bastard has moved in with that tramper, and they're living in Brunswick!" Mary seethed. "And now look at this. See what he's done! He's filed this—it's from his solicitor," she snarled, her mouth fuming, contorting and twisting itself into ugly shapes. For all her beauty, even Apollo didn't think his mother looked very attractive anymore. Apollo's face turned white as all the colour left his face. He felt drained. He couldn't believe what was happening; now the divorce really was coming through, and all hopes of his parents reconciling floated out the window. It had all become just too real for him. Apollo's head was spinning as he reflected on the last year; how just eleven short months earlier he had still been in his home country at his family home, with his friends and family and those he was comfortable with. He thought about this time, when his parents were still happy and together, and how everything had been so normal, stable and good. Fast forward less then a year later, and here he was, in a new country and a new school and new kids who hated him; he no longer had his father around, and now his parents were divorcing. It was all too much.

As the year came to a close, the bullying had also gotten so intense and random that no-one would speak up, not even the girls who had once crushed on Apollo. He was being bullied around the clock—and having no-one to turn to, and nowhere to go, and now no relationship with his father, Apollo started to hate everything about school and everything about life in general. He didn't want to get out of bed in the mornings now; he didn't want to eat; he didn't even want to play his beloved soccer games. He just wanted to disappear under the covers and never ever come out.

Meanwhile, Mary, oblivious to her son's heartache, had been out on the town and had now set her sights on a new man. Alan Benzeley was a sheriff's officer at the security company where she worked, and he towered over the little Greek Cypriots with his lithe, six-foot-two frame.

"I'd like you all to meet this wonderful man," Mary announced as she breezed into the kitchen one evening smelling like an entire bottle of perfume.

"Alan; these are my two sons, Apollo and Troy," she said, smiling that fake smile Apollo knew all too well. Yiayia was apparently thinking the same thing and abruptly got up from the table, politely excusing herself; she was wary of her daughter's decision to bring this man into their home, especially since she'd come home with her divorce papers just a few days earlier.

"Hello, boys, how you going—how's school going?" Alan asked. On the surface Apollo thought Alan seemed friendly enough, but both Apollo and Troy weren't up for any discussions, and they just wanted to make themselves scarce. They tried to bolt from the kitchen but Mary quickly blocked them.

"Wait—hey, you two, don't be so rude! This man is trying to be nice and be your friend here!" Mary yelled out, but Angela was quick to intervene on behalf of her two grandsons.

"Mary—" Yiayia politely interrupted, "They just need some time … don't you think?"

"Why, Mum? Why already a new man? Why so quick?" Troy jumped in.

Mary looked horrified and her face suddenly morphed into a

bright shade of pomegranate right there in front of her new beau. Alan, sensing her embarrassment, stepped in.

"Well, it's been great meeting you all, but I have to run—work calls," he said, winking at the boys, attempting to make an effort with them.

Angela gave the man a polite nod and asked Frank to come help her in the garden, thinking it best to pull back and leave them be. Mary turned to show Alan to the door.

"It's okay—they'll come around," Mary said breezily, reaching up on tiptoe and giving him a quick peck on the cheek.

CHAPTER SIX

An Australian Christmas

December 1986 was to be their first Australian Christmas, but as the year came to a close, Apollo just couldn't bring himself to feel the magic of Christmas or the usual merriment that accompanied it. The only light at the end of the tunnel (after being subjected to a year of bullying and humiliation) was that his friendship with Alora had grown from strength to strength; they were now so close that he considered her his girlfriend—though he'd been too shy to ever ask her, or make it official in any way.

Apollo spent Christmas Day with Yiayia and Papou and brother Troy; Alora was expected to come over in the late afternoon after spending time with her own family; and his mother and Alan would manage to make an appearance in the afternoon as well, long after the family had shared in the exchange of presents and when the afternoon's festivities were already well underway. Frank had organised the traditional lamb on the spit and some of the family's friends came to visit as well. Yiayia was busy in the kitchen cooking up a Greek feast of Cristopsomo, or 'Christ bread' of dough decorated with a cross, as well as cabbage leaf rolls filled with pork and spinach; then came the stuffed turkey and a big spinach and cheese pie. Finally the magnificent Vasilopita would ceremoniously emerge, to be cut and served; it was a Saint Basil's pie, the traditional dessert made for New Year's Day. Traditionally, every Vasilopita contains a coin, and the head of the family must cut the pie into pieces; whoever finds the coin is said to be in store for a lucky year. Frank got out his big carving knife and took the honours.

"Kala Cristougena, Merry Christmas," Apollo said and kissed his mother on the cheek. Troy followed suit, copying his big brother.

"Fröhliche weihnachten," this is how we say Merry Christmas in Deutschland, in Germany," Alan interrupted.

Apollo and Troy looked first at Alan, then at one another and grimaced. The boys didn't like or trust this man. He seemed cold, he rarely smiled, and he lacked any personality; on top of that, he only ever seemed to care about himself or the fact that he was proud of his German heritage. And right now it was painfully obvious that he revelled in any chance to discuss it.

"Well, we aren't German—we are proud Greek Cypriots!" little Troy boldly blurted out at the man. Who was this man anyway, and where was their father?

"Okay, boys, enough," Mary said, cutting them off and diverting them to their Christmas gifts. All the presents had been expertly wrapped in blue and white striped paper, and each tied with a satiny electric blue bow. All the colours of Greece. The boys dived into gift unwrappings, and Troy was excited to discover a new pack of computer games he'd been dying to play. They both got a new Nintendo game station to share and some new clothes and chocolates. Mary was elated when, after the boys had opened their presents, she discovered the coin in her pie.

"It's a sign! It's meant to be! I just knew my luck had turned," Mary glowed, turning to plant a big kiss on Alan's lips in front of everyone. Apollo felt like throwing up.

Overall, it had been a nice and pleasant enough day, but to Apollo it had also been a very strange day. The usual kalanda carol singing they did on the streets at Christmas Eve had disappeared, although Yiayia had worked to serve up the traditional pork roast and melomakarona, or honey cookies, the night before. Still, his parents followed the Gregorian calendar as faithfuls of the Greek Orthodox church, still deeply rooted in its traditions. Yiayia had decorated a small boat, which she said most Greek households did because it symbolised not only a love and respect for the sea, but the anticipation of reuniting with seafaring relatives and welcoming home one's long-lost loved ones. Yiayia began to tremble and then she teared up remembering her family, unable to contain her emotions any longer. Papou climbed out of his recliner and came to his wife's side.

"There, there, zoi mou, my wife, my life; this has been a hard year on all of us. Let us just be thankful we are all here in this great southern land we now call our home."

"I'm sorry Papou, I just—I just hoped things would be different this year ... This was supposed to be our first Christmas together; we were supposed to all be together," Yiayia sobbed. "It was why I grew my family in the first place, and to buy a big house like this. It's what we do, we Greeks live together so that we all stay close," she said, wiping her tears with her sleeve. "I feel like we need to burn the Cristoksilo logs in the fireplace, especially this year—to ward off the kalikanzari—or they will come and get us!" Yiayia cried, as she left Papou's side and started swinging her rosary beads around the room.

"What's wrong with Yiayia? What's kal-zik-arny?" Troy asked, concerned.

"It's kalikanzari—and it comes from a Greek legend that says that in the period between Christmas Eve and New Year there are harmful and mocking demonic creatures, called kalikanzari that can enter the house. If you burn Christmas logs in the fireplace it's believed you will be saved from them—"

"… and if we don't?" Troy asked, as a very real fear crossed his face.

"Look, boys—it's a legend, a myth. That's all. Besides, it's summertime here in Australia, and I'm not starting any crazy log fire. It's a fire hazard," Papou huffed.

"Okay, well we have to go now," Mary suddenly announced, getting up and giving Alan a look that said they were leaving. "We have to go and visit Alan's relatives on the other side of the city, in Brighton," she said, kissing Angela and Frank on the cheek.

"So soon? Why? You've only just eaten …" Yiayia said, looking hurt.

"… and Mum, I told you my new friend Alora was coming this afternoon, you promised you would be here to meet her?" Apollo complained sullenly.

"Sorry boys, but I can't be in two places at once—unless you'd like to split me in two," Mary quipped and kissed her boys on the cheek. "Now be good for Yiayia and Papou, and I will see you tomorrow," she said, abruptly scooping up her bag and making for the front door. Alan mumbled something that sounded like a departure but Apollo couldn't be bothered showing him any courtesies and went back in the living room to his presents.

Yiayia sat in the living room with her special wine Mary had brought her from Cyprus; she was reminiscing on the graves of her relatives, how at this time of year she used to lay down flowers for them and pray that the souls of the departed were resting in peace. She then started to tell the boys about their relatives and the second and third cousins who were still living back in Cyprus, when there came a knock at the door. Apollo leapt to his feet, instinctively guessing it was Alora. There she stood, waiting patiently by the front door and looking radiant in a blue floral dress and silver shoes. Her hair and makeup were done and she looked even more beautiful than she normally did at school. Apollo was speechless.

"Ah, hi—umm, please, come in and meet my family," Apollo gestured, executing his best, most gentlemanly manners. Alora blushed and stepped inside.

Troy waved in greeting, being more self-absorbed in his computer games, and Yiayia and Frank smiled warmly at the girl, welcoming her to their house.

"Ummm, yeah—well my Mum isn't here, she just left with her, umm, new boyfriend," Apollo announced with great difficulty, as though something were stuck in his throat about to make him choke.

"Oh, that's okay—I really just came to see you," Alora said, beaming happily. Apollo suddenly felt awkward; he always felt this way around girls. But he told himself to keep going because he really liked this girl. A lot.

"So … what did Aghios Vasilis, your Greek Santa, bring you this year?" Alora questioned him playfully.

"Oh you know … clothes, food, this and that … hey, wanna take a walk around the neighbourhood?" Apollo wanted to get away from everyone right now, because he felt too many pairs of eyes boring into him.

"Don't you want to offer the girl something to eat first? Some Vasilopita?" Yiayia suggested, getting up to serve more food.

"Oh, thank you—but I have already eaten too much today!" Alora laughed, and Apollo laughed along shyly with her. He felt so nervous and shy around her, but, at the same time, he felt strangely comfortable, too. It was refreshing to him that he could be himself, and here was someone who finally accepted him just for being him.

Alora handed Apollo a small basket of homemade halva her mother had made to give to the family; as they headed out the door, Yiayia nodded approvingly to Apollo. Yiayia had excellent radar, and she knew this was a good girl. Apollo smiled. Christmas had come and gone and Apollo and Alora walked a mile around the block together under the street lights, passing by the suburban Australian brick homes all decked out in colourful Christmas lights, pretty fake Christmas trees flickering and waving at them through the windows.

"So I guess you're not missing school much," Alora winked.

"There's only one thing about school I'm missing," Apollo winked back.

"So what are you going to do for the Christmas holidays?"

"Oh, my brother and I will probably hit the Coburg pools or the beach; I love the beach, the solitude—I find so much peace and harmony there. And it's a nice escape from … well, you know, everyday life ..." He knew Alora understood what he meant. Forget his struggles, forget troubles, forget everything ... and just let loose. He dreaded returning to school, to the bullying, the taunting, and he just wished he could say here forever. Like this. With Alora.

CHAPTER SEVEN

Sick Days

New Year's Eve came around and with no sign of Mary or Alan, New Year's was a quiet affair spent at his Yiayia and Papou's. It was an uneventful evening, and they all ate meat on the barbecue with a big Greek salad, then watched the festivities on TV for a while before retiring to bed.

By late January 1987, Troy and Apollo were both back in school, Troy in his final year of primary school and Apollo now in his second year of high school as a fully-fledged teenager. The year started out looking much like the previous year that would see Apollo constantly tormented and bullied. By midyear, the assistant principal, a lovely middle-aged woman named Rose Thornton, had seen enough of Apollo's constant struggles from a distance and had decided to get in touch with his mother, Mary, to arrange a meeting with her. But Mary was distracted by her new relationship and was sadly neglecting both of her boys' needs; and unaware of the issues Apollo was facing, sent his grandmother along to the meeting instead.

On July 17th, Angela attended the meeting with Rosa Thornton in her office also unaware of what the meeting was to be about. To her mind, Apollo was a model student who worked hard for his grades and was very studious.

"Mrs Pistakis, thank you for coming; I believe this meeting is very important, which is why I have called for it. We have to discuss certain things about your grandson, but I must admit I'm a little disappointed that their mother could not also be here today," Rose began, somewhat matter-of-factly. Rose's round face and soft features could easily have been mistaken for those of a maternal, motherly type of woman, but when it came to important matters like this, she was all business.

"I understand—and I am sorry my daughter could not also be here, but I am a little concerned and feeling rather apprehensive as to what this is all about," Angela replied, shaking.

"It's okay—it isn't anything to worry about, not as far as Apollo's having done anything wrong … Rather, it's something that needed to be brought to your—or more importantly, to his mother's—attention. You see, your grandson is not developing at the same rate as the rest of the students—and I feel he may be a late bloomer," Rose began gently.

"What do you mean by that? 'A late bloomer'?" Angela repeated, stupefied.

Mrs Thornton went on to explain that her son had had a similar problem and at one time had been short, skinny, underdeveloped and seemingly slower than the other students; but his problem had been identified early on, and with a loving home environment, and the right treatment and medical care he was able to overcome his developmental delays.

"We sent Joshua to be tested at the Royal Children's Hospital in

Melbourne for blood and bone work, and it's my professional recommendation that Apollo seek out similar testing and treatment."

Angela looked across the desk at Mrs Thornton with a stunned look on her face. She was shocked, because from what she could see, never once had Angela noticed anything that was wrong with Apollo. Yes, he could be considered a little on the short side—but weren't most Greeks? And height certainly didn't run in their family. Still, Rose insisted that Apollo should be sent to be tested and checked for his development, just to make sure he was okay and on the up and up, at the level end of his development. Rose smiled warmly then and gave Angela a contact card with a phone number.

"Thank you for this," Angela said sincerely; she was eternally grateful for Rose's help and she took the card and put it in her purse.

"There is just one more thing … I'm sure it's nothing and Apollo is fine—and I wouldn't say anything to him about it, either—but I've seen a bit of teasing being directed at him in the playground. Again, I wouldn't suggest saying anything to Apollo, especially if he hasn't already mentioned it to you; but I will keep an eye on things at my end, and please let me know if you notice anything different in his behaviour. Of course, these are the difficult teenage years, and as we know most of the time these things sort themselves out. Plus, he is a very fine student, a very bright young man, and one of our best at this school," Rose added reassuringly.

"Thank you, I will do that," Angela said, shaking Mrs Thornton's hand.

When Apollo came home after school, Troy was already home playing video games after having done his homework. Angela called out to Apollo in Greek, asking him to come out to the kitchen. Apollo put his school bag in his room and came out to greet Yiayia.

Απόλλων, ελάτε στην κουζίνα και μιλήστε με την Yiayia!

Apollo, come to the kitchen and talk to Yiayia!

"What's up? Everything okay?" Apollo asked, reaching for a slice of halloumi and dipping a dolmathes, stuffed and rolled grape leaves in a bowl of Greek yoghurt.

"Yes darling, I just needed to talk to you, so why don't you sit down and I will make you and your brother some keftethes," Yiayia said, busying herself at the stove. Apollo sat down and Angela started cooking the sizzling meatballs and talking at the same time.

"So I met up with Mrs Thornton today, and she was very pleasant and helpful in bringing to my attention that you might have a development problem," she said, trying to sound nonchalant. Just then, Frank arrived home, having finished a session at the swim-spa-sauna, and Mary was off with Alan shopping, having now completely abandoned her responsibilities as a mother. Angela put down her wooden spoon for a minute to explain to both Apollo and Frank what the assistant principal had told her that afternoon.

"It's nothing to go be alarmed about—Mrs Thornton is a very nice lady, and she has experience with this because her own son had some difficulty with his growth spurts too. In fact—" she said, looking to Frank to back her up, "your mother also had some developmental problems growing up, too, so quite often it's something found to be hereditary, genetically passed on."

Apollo felt sad because he didn't want there to be anything wrong with him, or for there to be yet something else that he could potentially be teased about, so he readily agreed to Yiayia making a phone call to the Royal Children's Hospital and to an appointment the following week. Alora arrived shortly thereafter and she and Apollo went out to the movies at Northland Shopping Centre, because *Predator* was playing at the cinemas. Apollo was so grateful for Alora; she was the one positive thing in his life right now and the one constant, what with the bullying, the estranged relationship with his parents, and missing his home country and friends back in Cyprus. Alora was the one steady, shining light that he looked forward to, and it kept him going, along with his beloved grandparents.

"What a great movie that was!" Alora beamed, finishing off the last of the popcorn as they sat reclining in their seats. Apollo nodded; he suddenly fell quiet, wondering whether to tell Alora about the hospital visit. In the end, he decided against it; they were having such a lovely night together that he didn't want to ruin anything.

The following week however, Apollo went to the Royal Children's Hospital with Yiayia, disheartened that his own mother was never home; rather, she was spending most of her time with the new beau, Alan. It hurt him to think that she didn't care, and it made him feel as though he didn't matter to her anymore. Apollo sat in the waiting room with Yiayia, who told more stories of her childhood in Cyprus. Apollo loved listening to her stories so much, and it really was the one and only thing that could distract him and calm his nerves before he heard his name being called out by the medical staff. He looked at Yiayia and suddenly felt worried; what if the doctors found something wrong with him? Yiayia smiled at her grandson; of course she loved both her grandsons, but she especially loved Apollo with all her heart.

"You will be okay, my child, and I will be right here waiting for you. Nothing bad is going to happen."

The doctor introduced himself as Doctor Stevenson. He was a tall professor from Oxford University, a very polite and friendly man.

"So, Apollo! How are you today? We got your referral letter and … let's see here … you are thirteen, correct? Thirteen, hmmm, but seemingly a slow developer—and there are concerns over your weight and height, and all round wellbeing? Is that correct, mate?"

Apollo nodded nervously with a despondent, "Yes Sir, I think so."

"Okay, then let's get you to jump on those scales, mate, and we'll check your weight; once you're done we will check your height measurements too."

Apollo did all that was needed in following the doctor's instructions, then he was sent off to the radiology department so they could perform the necessary blood work and bone X-rays. Apollo sat shivering on the edge of the gurney in his medical gown; the hospital was cold and white and he hated being there, but he also knew it was for the best. He chuckled to himself, thinking how Gavin Croosy must be waiting for him at the school gates while he knew he would never show up. *Ha! Stupid Croosy,* he thought. Dr Stevenson left to examine the test results and Apollo sat there waiting for him for what seemed like forever. Soon enough, several new doctors Apollo had never seen came through the glass doors to discuss Apollo's results, but Apollo couldn't hear anything except the muffled sounds of deliberations coming from the other side of the room. Dr Stevenson then excused himself and stepped outside to take a phone call, and Apollo sat there shivering for what seemed like an eternity.

Finally, the doctors all reconvened in the room; whatever it was they had discussed Apollo now braced himself for, but he was finally ready to hear it.

"Well, Apollo; it seems as if you may in fact have some stunted growth going on here; the doctors and I have discussed the possibility of injections, which we feel would greatly assist you in putting you back on track with your continued development. I've had a very close look at the results myself, however—" he leaned over Apollo and put the chart down, "we can't do anything without your help—you have to be a willing patient, and be willing to do the work, too."

Apollo became tearful then; he didn't like needles and didn't know how he was going to cope with having a needle daily.

"Don't worry, I know what you're thinking—I don't like needles myself," he chuckled sympathetically. "But if you don't take it, you won't get better. Right?" Doctor Stevenson then asked him to stand in the corner. "Now Apollo, I want you to jump up and down until I tell you to stop. On the count of three: Go."

Apollo obeyed and started jumping up and down on the spot repeatedly. He kept up a fast pace until, after several minutes he couldn't continue any longer and he doubled over, clutching at his knees and calves in pain. The Doctor glanced over at him.

"Are you feeling any pain in your legs, Apollo?"

"Yes," Apollo admitted reluctantly. "Yes, they hurt."

Doctor Stevenson stood up and in a stern voice told the other doctors that Apollo was fine and didn't—and wouldn't—be taking any injections. Apollo would have jumped for joy right then and there if his legs hadn't hurt him so much. Relief swept through his entire body as he realised he also wouldn't have to have any injections. Nothing was wrong with him! Nothing! The kids at school had always made him feel like a leper, a hunchback; yet here he was being told by a doctor that he was fine—and even better than fine—normal! It was music to Apollo's ears, and it was the best news he could have ever hoped for, and immediately he felt his muscles relax as relief swept over his entire being. Normal. He was normal. What a lovely word that was.

"Yes," Dr Stevenson repeated back to Apollo, your development is normal. But your development is slower, about four years slower, than the average child in your age group; but this is normal too, because all children develop at varying rates and speeds. As for the pain in your legs—these are growing pains—and we will be able to give you some natural tablets, supplements for you to take, which will aid you in speeding up your development. The good news here, Apollo, is that you do not need any steroid injections, which I believe would hinder and negatively affect your structure in any case."

Apollo felt so relieved and grateful; he loved this doctor so much he could have just jumped up and hugged him right then and there. Angela saw her grandson's face break into a great big smile as soon as he returned to the waiting room, and then she too broke into a great big smile; Apollo wrapped his grandmother up in a big bear hug through happy tears.

"Hello, Angela; well we are lucky to have this positive result today; please understand it will be difficult going for a little while, and patience will be a virtue as we get Apollo going on the right medications; but in time I believe everything will work out well for him," Dr Stevenson reassured her. "An idea, Apollo—you might want to consider taking up some form of martial arts, it's great for bone strengthening and self-confidence; also, increase your iron intake, as this builds strong and healthy bones for a young man like yourself."

Apollo and Angela returned home with his new prescriptions; when they arrived, there was Troy playing video games with a few of his friends, and Frank was out in the garden tending to his vegetables. Apollo turned the corner into the living room and was shocked to see his mother sitting there on the couch with Alan, being all cosy and cuddly and intimate together. It had been weeks since she had been home, and Apollo felt his face burning up at the sight of her. Upon seeing Apollo, she quickly stood up and rushed to greet him.

"Oh, my Apollo! It's lovely to see you! Now everyone, please come gather in the living room, because I have something very important to tell you all!" Mary spun about giddily clapping her hands together, her long luscious hair falling softly around her face as Frank and Yiayia made their way into the room. Alan stood up and took his place by Mary's side, looking smug.

"Wait! Wait! Okay, are you all ready—Alan proposed to me last night—he has asked me to marry him—and I said: Yes!" she beamed excitedly like a schoolgirl. Angela glanced at her husband, then over to Apollo and Troy. Troy's eyes were so wide his pupils dilated. Frank was aghast that his daughter could be moving so quickly; they hardly knew the man. Plus, he wasn't a Greek.

"Mary, we need to talk—"

"Not now, Mum—it's my time to shine now … We can talk later tonight when we get back from shopping and a movie; Alan is taking me out now to pick out an engagement ring!"

Whoa. Apollo just stood there looking stunned and feeling mortified. How come this was now all about her when he had just spent the whole day at the hospital without her because she hadn't been bothered enough to go? Apollo was silently fuming inside. However, in the moment, Mary took her son's reaction merely as one of surprise, and was subsequently puzzled when Apollo simply turned and left the room without saying a word.

"They'll come round, eventually," she said, nervously trying to laugh it off and flipping through the pages of a magazine in front of her.

That night, Mary didn't come home as promised, but called Angela to explain that she was busy and would be home in the next couple of days. Angela didn't really mind; she loved her grandsons and having them with her meant the world to her; but even Yiayia had to admit she was completely surprised by her daughter's lack of understanding when it came to her own children. Yet Yiayia felt stuck; she couldn't say anything, because she didn't want to have to deal with any confrontation with her only daughter, who she knew could be hot-headed and strong-willed at the best of times. Yiayia put it down to it being an extension of her fiery and passionate blood line the Greeks were known for. And, besides, what was the point of making ripples, Yiayia thought, always seeing the bigger picture; here they were, finally all together as one big Greek family in the same country. That was what mattered the most. Family. So Yiayia let the matter slide and instead, went to work preparing dinner for the boys. Besides, they had something to celebrate and toast to tonight: Apollo's good health.

CHAPTER EIGHT

Opa!

Alora was coming over after school more often now, and she and Apollo were getting closer, despite the fact that the bullying was still going on. Gavin Croosy, Cale Moss and Simon Libb continued with their daily taunts, tormenting and humiliating Apollo in discreet locations of the school, their lithe, tall and skinny frames bearing down on him, cornering him in dead end corridors whenever they could. Apollo fought hard to avoid them, but there were always the off days where he would become caught between a rock and a hard place as they cordoned him off in a far corner of the school grounds, and their cunningness always worked a treat. They deliberately overpowered Apollo, leaving him feeling fragile, weak and small, until he hated going to school altogether.

By November 1987, Mary and Alan were busy preparing their wedding day; Mary announced that the ceremony would be held at a Greek Orthodox church in Fawkner, while for the reception she had chosen a quaint venue in Eltham, a pretty and rustic Australian town just outside of the city, because it had a country feel to it. This surprised Yiayia because it had not been what she was expecting; she thought her daughter, being as extravagant as she was, would want another big Greek wedding, as big and as expensive as her first wedding had been to Mateus.

"Oh no, Mama—I don't want to frighten Alan or scare him off. It would ruin everything! Besides, he doesn't want the whole big Greek wedding thing, it's just not him … we want something more modern, more … Australian," Mary said, playing down her Greekness. With only a week to go, Mary insisted on having a family meeting over dinner with her parents to iron out the final details. Apollo asked if he could invite Alora to dinner too; as hard as it was going to be, he thought it was time Alora finally met his mother. Apollo had told Alora everything, from moving from Cyprus, to his parents splitting up, to his father Mateus, who was now long gone from the picture and had stopped contacting his boys, having taken up with a new woman, Olivia, who now had all of his attention. The falling out with both his parents had come at the worst possible time in his life; however, Troy was definitely faring better than his older brother because he had no developmental problems or bullying issues to contend with, and being much younger, he just didn't remember as much, nor see as much as Apollo did.

"So, are you seeing my son?" Mary began, as she sat down at the table opposite Apollo and Alora, a fake smile covering her face. Her words rang out in a slightly patronising undertone in her weak attempt to break the ice. Apollo bit back, sounding curt.

"Yes, she is—and it's none of your business," he retorted, his face showing signs of anger. Alora reached out and put her hand on Apollo's arm under the table as Alan pursed his lips, ready to say something, but Angela intervened and quickly changed the subject back to the wedding plans, which was a very clever and effective way of distracting Mary. Apollo thought his mother was easy like that; she was like a dog, so easy to distract with a bone, or morsels of food, or anything pertaining to herself. Alora knew full well everything that had happened in the family plus the level of family dysfunction going on, and she vowed to sit quietly by Apollo's side in solidarity.

"Is she Greek? She looks Greek … good then," Mary stated, sizing Alora up with her eyes. Apollo cringed. He wished the earth would swallow him up whole right then, but Alora took it all in stride and just smiled. He was ecstatic that he had a blossoming relationship with Alora, this beautiful girl who was fast developing into a young woman, and he was petrified at what his mother was capable of doing to ruin it. His self-confidence and self-esteem issues had taken enough of a beating lately without the additional problems caused by a poor family home life, and so he guarded his relationship with Alora, because to him it was as sacred as his belief in God.

"So you never did tell us how you two met," Alora quizzed Mary in return. Mary was all ready to talk wedding plans, but this girl seemed feisty, more like herself, she thought, and was far from the shy and delicate wallflower she felt her son was turning into.

"Well, he was someone I had met while out shopping; Alan had noticed me many times, apparently, and he started making trips to the local shops—"

"Yes," Alan joined in, "I was hoping to catch her in town somewhere, and then I saw her working at the security company where I worked, and—"

"—and I wasn't really interested, after my recent breakup and all; but he was sooo persistent!" Mary exclaimed gleefully.

"Yes, when I want something, I go for it," Alan bragged, ogling Mary's exposed cleavage resting just above the table.

"Oh, Alan!" Mary exclaimed, titillated. "Well, he did move very fast—in the first week he bought me a gorgeous necklace that said, 'Agapi Mou' which, as you know means 'my love' in Greek. Then, to seal the deal, he proposed a few weeks later, asking me if I'd be his wife. After a few minutes of ugly crying I said yes! How old are you, Alora? Fifteen? Maybe before too long my Apollo will propose to you, too!" Mary teased.

"Mama stop!" Apollo blurted out, frustrated. He couldn't believe how cruel she was being; he felt she was deliberately trying to embarrass him now. Apollo had had enough; he politely asked Yiayia if he and Alora could be excused from the table and Yiayia readily agreed, freeing Apollo and Alora to bolt to his room.

"You shouldn't do that to the poor child, Mary," Yiayia scolded her daughter. "He's not a child anymore—he's becoming a young man, and you'd do well to respect this."

"Oh Mama, lighten up. We were just having fun," Mary cried, helping herself to a serving of lamb kebabs and pita bread. "Apollo's just too sensitive; he needs to toughen up is all," she said, chewing on her lamb.

***

The wedding day almost upon them, Mary had beautiful dresses for the bridesmaids to choose with a styling brief of structured lace; the flowers were a muted arrangement of greenery, which included Australian eucalypts, olive and Italian ruscus and mostly white flowers of delphiniums, roses, lisianthus, hydrangea, eryngium and peonies. She didn't want anything too loud or colourful, as she'd wanted to create more of the soft whites reminiscent of her native country, mixed with Australian flora.

After the zomata or traditional 'getting ready' ceremony, which involved the bridal party partaking in a fertility ritual, it was time for Mary's single friends to write their names on the soles of her shoes, another Greek tradition that held the belief that whoever's name remained there and didn't get smudged off after all the dancing by the end of the night would be the next to marry. The bridesmaids then tied red ribbons and decorations to the newlywed's marital bed, throwing money, small gifts and rice for prosperity.

Then it was time for the bride to step out in all her splendour. Mary appeared, a Greek goddess dressed all in white; as they arrived at the church she stepped out of the limousine, her long train and embroidered veil floating in the warm November breeze. The wedding guests gasped, taken in by her sheer beauty, her soft dark hair falling down around her shoulders as she walked. Yiayia cried happy tears as a violinist serenaded her upon Mary's entrance; she could not believe her daughter was getting married again. The priest was waiting for them both at the end of the aisle; he adorned their heads with the traditional stefani crowns, two rings made of silver and gold and attached by a ribbon, signifying the couple as the now unified king and queen of their home. After the marrying prayer the ceremony was complete, and the priest blessed the couple in their crowns, ensuring a blissful life together; he then encouraged Mary to stomp on her husband's foot, a symbol of the woman's power over the man, that she should have the upper hand in the marriage.

"Ouch! That hurt!" Alan wailed, and the wedding guests all laughed.

They exited the church as husband and wife, where the guests were required to fake spit on them three times for good luck and throw more rice in what soon turned into a rice war. Then, it was time for the celebrations to begin, and all the guests followed the married couple in a procession of cars to the reception hall to get the party started. It was a stunning venue, and Alora reached out for Apollo's hand as they entered a room filled with vases of large floral arrangements while candles flickered and burned brightly in clear lanterns and low-light festoons. Even Apollo had to admit he was impressed by it all.

"Oh my God!" Alora exclaimed, breathless. "This is just so beautiful and romantic!" Apollo had to stop and study her profile then, and saw her perfect features and fine porcelain skin in the flicker of candlelight. Right then and there, Apollo knew once and for all he had become truly besotted with this girl.

They feasted the way Greeks do at big Greek weddings, on a smorgasbord of Greek delights that ranged from village salads to plates of halloumi, souvlaki finger foods, roast pork and more. The wedding cake was a simple and unadorned vanilla sponge cake large enough to feed them all; with an assortment of other sweet Greek treats there was so much dessert no-one could finish it all.

The music began, and Mary took to the dance floor to dance with her father. Frank guided her gently around the room to *Butterfly Kisses,* Mary's favourite, and a song her Baba had sung to her when she was little. Yiayia sat and sobbed in the corner; in fact, she cried so hard she wept as Greek mothers do, as though she was never going to see her daughter again, despite the fact that they were living in the same house. It was the same for all Greeks, Apollo thought, and he got up to put a comforting arm around his grandmother.

"Oh, Apollo," she said, "You are my good Greek boy. I am so proud of you."

Then the big Greek band started to play Laika and Rembetika, and in no time at all, the wedding had turned into a bouzoukia scene. Knowing how much the Greeks love to dance, the entire bridal party swamped the dance floor and formed a circle, for the traditional dances of the Tsamiko, the Zeibekkiko and the Sirtaki, which really got the party going. They all held hands and jumped about, the men waving white napkins overhead as the women jiggled in the middle, giving everyone a show of their dance skills. A few men even kneeled to show off their partners while they snapped their fingers and clapped in celebration.

The night just got crazier and crazier as people danced and sang and threw flowers at the singers; in one corner a guy was balancing what looked like over twenty-five glasses on his head! Apollo and Alora danced away, sneaking sips of ouzo when the parents were not watching, and then it was announced that the kefi, or plate smashing, would start soon. Kefi was a well known custom at Greek Cypriot weddings or any happy occasion; guests threw plates like frisbees, smashing them to express all the joy and passion that life brings.

"Opa! Opa!" They all screamed as everyone danced and got more and more drunk on booze.

Finally, Alan's father tinkled his glass and everyone quieted down for the speeches.

"The day is finally here," he announced to a room full of people. "To Alan and Mary! May you both live a long and happy life together!"

In typical Greek fashion, it wasn't a Greek wedding until all the guests were well and truly drunk; the music got louder as the guests became louder and by the time it came to the last dance of the night people were all falling over each other, and Apollo was laughing so hard his sides hurt. All the guests were either half-dead from all the food and drink or passed out in a corner. Troy was giggly on beer in one corner, and in another, Yiayia was speaking Greek to the older guests.

The final dance was Mary and Alan's; as they started to dance, all the guests started throwing money at the couple and pinning money to their backs. "Opa! Opa!" they all cried out again, and soon everyone was on the dance floor, forming a circle and waving their napkins, wishing them well in their married life.

The night came to a close and Mary could be seen kissing the cheeks of her guests as, one by one, they filed out.

"Ke Sta Dika Su, Ke Sta Dika Su," she said to her single friends, a traditional wish for them to marry and find happiness, too. Everyone received bombonieres, almond candy favours, as a sign of thanks upon their departure, and Mary kicked off her heels, complaining about her feet after so many hours of dancing.

The whole evening went rather well, with all the family and friends who'd attended saying what a wonderful time they'd had. But a Greek wedding could never be fully Greek without at least one embarrassing moment because Greeks never fail to embarrass each other.

The photographer was making the final rounds with his camera, snapping happy pictures of the event, and he made his way over to the happy couple, asking them for a few final group photos. By this stage Mary was well and truly drunk, and she yelled out at the top of her lungs to her new in-laws Alva, Alan's mother, and Henry, Alan's stepfather.

"Alva! Henry! Come over here: we need a picture with you!"

she cried, her crown and veil toppling off the side of her head. Apollo and Troy were standing close by, and Troy offered to reach up and reaffix his mother's crown. Apollo stood nearby, thinking he would be called to be in the picture too, so he stood there and patiently waited for his mother to straighten her appearance. The photographer instructed them to gather and squeeze in together for the shot, and Apollo, thinking he had to shuffle more into the frame, moved closer to his mother ready for the picture to be taken.

"No! No, Apollo! You can't be in this picture—this is only for the adults! You go sit over there, and I'll be there in a minute." This was her day, Mary reasoned; and her children weren't to ruin it.

CHAPTER NINE

Bully for You

One minute Apollo was the centre of his mother's world; the next, he was a forgotten piece of furniture. At the turn of another year, 1988 looked bright for Alan and Mary as they had returned from a glorious two-week honeymoon to Bali and starting their new life. Meanwhile, Apollo faced new struggles at school in the form of more bullying and now diminishing grades. Apollo was now at an all-time low; his developmental delays and stress at school inevitably led to his inability to focus on his schoolwork, and his education began to suffer.

It didn't help matters that his mother was completely oblivious to the events of the past year with regards to her boys; but it was now clear to everyone around them that Mary was neglecting her motherly duties and obligations, and the welfare and wellbeing of her children was at stake: they were suffering. Apollo was taking his daily medications for his developmental delays, but when he compared himself to the other boys at school, he thought his arms looked skinny and wiry, his chest cavity was not filling out like theirs, and at fifteen, he still had barely a hair on his body. The one thing that looked good were his running legs; although short, they were toned and well-defined, as though they had been carved out of something like an Adonis sculpture. He was still developing; it was just slow.

Meanwhile, Troy had had a growth spurt of his own and was shooting up like a beanstalk, fast catching up to his brother. This did nothing for Apollo's already fragile self-esteem and low self-confidence. Troy came up to Apollo in the kitchen one morning and casually slung his arm around his brother's neck.

"How's it hanging, bro?" Troy asked in his usual easygoing manner. But all Apollo could think of was how his younger brother now met with him at shoulder level; before too long, he realised, Troy would be towering over him in the height department, and this depressed Apollo to no end. Troy had also turned a corner into his teens, and upon starting high school he'd gotten in with a crowd that liked to smoke behind the school canteen.

"Hey, is that short dude your brother, man? I can't believe you guys are related," one kid commented, puffing on a cigarette. Troy felt himself caught between embarrassment and wanting to stand up for his brother, so he told the kid to shut the fuck up and give him another drag of his cigarette. Troy loved his brother. He knew and understood his brother's developmental problems, but he didn't care; to him, Apollo was his funny, sweet, goofy brother, and no-one could ever know or understand the million miles they'd travelled together, and this gave them a special bond that could never be broken. Plus, Troy would never experience being bullied in the way that Apollo had; he could handle himself in a crowd and knew how to hold his own.

Mary continued to revel in her budding relationship and new marriage to Alan. They had even moved into the back room at Yiayia and Frank's large home, although there had been no prior discussion about this, and this made things awkward for Frank and Angela and the boys. But Frank and Angela loved their daughter and would do what was required to keep the family together and keep the peace even though it would come at a cost.

The boys were happy enough that their mother was home again, but sadly, Mary was never around; she was always either working at the security company, skipping out for drinks with friends or getting her hair and nails done to look good for Alan. Mary was too caught up in her own little world to care; as far as she was concerned, she was married now, and it was all about the title and respect. After her most recent divorce, she would hold on tight to this man and their new relationship as best as she could; and, if that meant sacrificing her sons in the meantime, then so be it. On a deeper level, Yiayia sensed that Mary's divorce from Mateus had hit her hard, and Angela and Frank could see it; they knew their daughter, and her fear of being alone or abandoned, they sensed, was the reason she'd thrown herself prematurely into another relationship in the first place as they'd seen her do many times before. What they hadn't seen coming were the hints of a borderline personality disorder bubbling to the surface; as her response to things became more and more explosive, Mary was quicker to anger, and she got snappy and short with everyone around her, and this was another early sign that all was not well with Mary.

Apollo was spending more and more time on the athletics field because that was now preferable to being at home around his mother and Alan. It still made him feel awkward seeing them together; the way they flirted playfully in the kitchen as she cooked him breakfast, or to see them cuddled up together on the sofa watching TV. It made Apollo sad too, that his father had completely disappeared out of his life, and he had to question whether his father had ever loved him at all. These thoughts consumed Apollo, and it turned him into a fireball of energy as he burned around the track, his strong running legs carrying him faster and faster. When he came home from school, Apollo felt so lethargic and depleted he just wanted to fall into a giant heap. Only Alan was home, because Mary had gone out shopping for new bed linen and Frank and Yiayia had gone off to their weekly bingo game.

"You need to go take a shower, boy," Alan said to Apollo when he first walked into the kitchen to get a drink of water that he liked to squeeze with lemon.

"Yeah, I will—I'm just going to get a drink and relax first," Apollo said casually, feeling exhausted.

But Alan suddenly became forceful and aggressive. "No—I said you need to take a shower now, not later," he said, starting to sound militant. Apollo didn't like the sudden change in Alan's voice, which unnerved him.

"My Yiayia doesn't tell me when I have to shower—" Apollo pushed back, trying to stand up to him. He was so sick and tired of being bullied.

"Well, do I look like Yiayia? I'm not Yiayia—and I just told you to go shower! Now do as I say!" he barked, coming up to Apollo and standing over him, his fists clenched. Feeling powerless now, Apollo felt he could do nothing, so he just gave Alan a greasy disgusted look and spun off on his heels to the bathroom. Who did this guy think he was, coming in and taking charge and controlling everything just like that, anyway? Apollo stood under the hot steam of the shower, his hatred soaring for this man, this complete stranger who was now in his home. He decided to lock himself in his room and do his homework until Yiayia and Frank came home, until he could hear her clanging about in the kitchen getting pots out in preparation for making stew for dinner.

"Hey Yiayia, how was bingo?" Apollo greeted his grandmother, wrapping his arms around her while shooting a cold look over at Alan.

"Your Papou and I didn't win, but our lucky numbers did come up—twice!" she bragged happily as she started slicing the onions.

Troy and Mary were the next to arrive home; Mary had seen Troy walking down the street and picked him up along the way, giving him a ride. Yiayia asked if they'd be joining them for dinner. Mary nodded, but Troy shook his head.

"Sorry, Yiayia, I've got Nintendo night with my mates," Troy said, skipping out the door again.

Over dinner, Alan quickly tried to take charge and control of the household and spoke to Frank as though he were the authority on every subject. Apollo could see the way he was moving in, not only on his mother but the entire family. The Germans were known for being dogmatic and forward, and Apollo felt this man's nasty agenda a mile off like a dog's rear end.

So, the first few months of 1988, Apollo knew to steer clear of Alan whenever he was around; but, at other times, he became stuck around him when nobody else was home. Whenever Frank and Angela were out at bingo, or his mother was off shopping, Alan started to throw his weight around, ordering the boys to do chores or eat at certain times, shower at certain times. Often he used his weight and size to his advantage too, and tried to intimidate the boys, mainly Apollo, who was the most resistant to Alan's effrontery. They became like oil and water, and one day when Apollo wouldn't instantly jump on command, Alan blew up like a dust storm.

"I'll fucking hurt you if you don't listen to me!" Alan screamed at Apollo, the veins protruding in his neck.

Apollo now saw the man and his true colours, even if he hadn't before. Alan was a bully, a loser, and a narcissist who thrived on easy, smaller targets, and his true colours were coming to the fore. There was a reason why he didn't like this man from the get-go, and now he could see why—Apollo already had a deep and educated understanding of what bullying looked like at any age, and he was having nothing more of it.

For months on end, Alan would control the household discreetly, always when Apollo was alone and always when Mary, Troy, Yiayia or Frank weren't around. As soon as they stepped in the house Alan would suddenly shift gears and change his tune to that of a loving, devoted husband.

"Hi honey, how was your day?" Alan asked sweetly, his voice soft and smooth. He would smirk back at Apollo over his shoulder, as if to say, 'Don't mess with me, kid,' and Apollo felt so sick to his stomach he would retreat to his bedroom, his safe place, rather than having to deal with any more head games played by the likes of Alan. However, Yiayia did notice her grandson becoming quieter of late; and it made her think about contacting Mrs Thornton, who had asked her to keep watch over any changes in Apollo's behaviour.

Things had in fact become so bad that Apollo didn't feel he could invite Alora over for fear of being ridiculed or embarrassed by Alan. He made excuses to her instead, saying she could come later when he knew Yiayia or Papou would be home to safeguard him. Alora saw Apollo withdrawing and becoming more and more distant, but she put it down to the fact that the three bullies, Cale, Gavin, and Simon had been on him like never before because of their recent growth spurt, turning them into even larger, stronger monsters than before.

"What's wrong, Apollo? Please, can you talk to me?" Alora pleaded, trying to reach him. But Apollo said nothing, because there was nothing he could do. He just couldn't understand what had happened to his once loving mother, that she would put them all in this situation; yet he didn't feel safe enough to broach the subject, even with her. He just felt as if the whole world hated him.

Apollo would suffer in silence with his new stepfather, even though he was completely aware now of his manipulative ways. The man was a master manipulator, able to switch gears and put on a nice show for his new in-laws, even playing the nice father figure to Apollo and Troy whenever Frank and Angela were both home; but only Apollo knew the real Alan behind closed doors.

"Come here," Alan would say, taunting Apollo whenever he came home from school. This was now the norm, and Apollo felt he had nowhere to run. When Apollo wasn't looking, Alan crept up behind him one day, putting a plastic bag over Apollo's face and head and securing it tightly at the base with his two hands.

"Haha! Let's see how long you can hold your breath," Alan said, tormenting him. Apollo struggled against him, gasping for air. When his lips had turned blue, Alan let go his stronghold over the boy, and released the bag. Apollo doubled over in shock, wheezing and crying onto the floor. He didn't dare answer Alan back, for fear he might do something worse.

"Ah, stop being a crybaby! You gotta grow yourself some balls," was all Alan said as he sauntered away, lighting a cigarette.

Three days later Alan was at it again, up to his old tricks as he pounced on Apollo out of the blue, shoving his head in Apollo's face, trying to intimidate him, always when no-one was around. Apollo would curl into his own skin in fright, and Alan would just mutter 'chicken shit' at him and walk away.

Apollo was a fast learner, and whilst his grades had diminished, along with his home life and his schooling being still borderline, it was again Alora who was the one constant that kept him going, alongside Yiayia and Papou, who were always there, giving him hope and encouragement. One day, Angela came home early, as she had been expecting a parcel that was arriving any day now. To her shock and horror, she arrived upon the scene just in time to witness Alan grabbing Apollo by the throat and swirling him around the kitchen table before slamming him, head first, into her tiled benchtop. Angela screamed as she raced over to Alan, digging her nails deep into his neck, forcing him to release his grip on her grandson. He turned around and Yiayia slapped him hard with a loud clap, square across his jawline, all the while screaming hysterically.

"I will kill you if you EVER touch my grandson again, do you hear me?!"

Mary came running into the kitchen screaming at her mother not to interfere, when Apollo, enraged at his own mother for defending the brute instead of her own flesh and blood, let loose on her with his own words of hatred.

"He isn't my father! I will eat and go to bed when I want, but this cunt has no right to interfere in our family—and you are a slut and a bitch of a mother and I just don't know you anymore!"

Apollo screamed at the top of his lungs. Angela was horrified at what was transpiring, and Frank held onto her arm, protecting his wife, unable to speak. Even mild mannered Frank was at boiling point.

"How LONG has this been happening?" Yiayia suddenly demanded, challenging Alan, eyeball to eyeball; but Apollo jumped in and took it upon himself to answer.

"Ever since he married her—and every time you and Papou leave to go anywhere outside of the house, he is a bastard and he bullies us!" Apollo was so vengeful and so angry in this moment that he felt he was screaming at everyone who had ever hurt him.

Alan tried to talk over Apollo then, but Angela raised her hand, suddenly shushing him.

"You will keep quiet right now—because this is my house and you're no longer welcome here if you ever touch Apollo again, do you understand me? Do I make myself clear? And, as for you, Mary—" Angela said, spinning around to face her daughter, "What kind of a mother are you anyway, to allow this? Aren't you ashamed of yourself? To call yourself a mother?" Angela was done. Finished. She was so disgusted with them both that she stormed out of the room, slamming the door. Troy came into the kitchen and shook his head; he didn't think Alan was too bad, but then again, being younger and not the easy target had made things so much easier for him.

From that moment on, Angela decided that she would stay home more often, and if she ever went shopping then she would insist on taking Apollo with her, even to bingo.

***

Two years they'd been in Australia now, and while everything was not going according to plan, Apollo knew he had found a rare treasure in Alora. Alora was a good month older than Apollo, and on December 31st, she closed in on him at the family's New Year's gathering. In the festivities of the night, she sidled up to Apollo with a wine in her hand, fondly teasing him as she towered over him in shiny red heels.

"You are so cute and so short," she smirked playfully, teasing his hair and gently stroking his face. For over a year now they had been hanging out almost daily, mostly as close friends, and they'd spent most of their time watching movies or playing video games in between school and studying; but now they were growing, changing, and growing closer in new ways as they matured. In the final seconds counting down into a new year they stood out on the front porch together, and Alora leaned in, pulling in Apollo for their first kiss. It was slow and tender, and as meaningful as Apollo had always hoped it would be. He was smitten. As they pulled back gently, Alora smiled and looked at him, blushing as she took in his striking features, looking into the kindest and loveliest eyes she had ever seen. She took his hand and they went back inside to join the others, their union sealed in a kiss. For all the ugliness of the year that had passed, Apollo thought, everything in this one moment made it all worth it, made it all right again. Alora stayed the night, staying up late into the wee hours talking with Yiayia and Papou, who found her to be the most polite and delightful girl, too.

"I really like them," Alora commented, after Yiayia and Papou had retired to bed.

"They really like you," Apollo said and took her hands in his.

"It was such a memorable New Year's …"

"Alora, I'd like to meet your family," Apollo said suddenly, with utmost seriousness.

"Soon, my darling, soon," she replied, kissing his soft, full lips. He was so kissable.

Mary and Alan were nowhere to be seen, and though Yiayia was disappointed that the whole family weren't together, at the same time, she felt relieved. She was not good at confrontation, and after all the destruction she had seen in her own country, she just wanted peace.

"Do you think Mary and Alan will come back? Yiayia was very upset tonight," Alora noted. Apollo just shrugged, he had had enough talking about it. But Alora pressed on.

"When Papou came in the room tonight and said he was proud of you for standing up to Alan and was sorry he hadn't seen the signs earlier with regards to Alan, he said that Yiayia had filled him in on what had been happening months back. What was that about?"

Apollo, not wanting to tell Alora how Alan had been bullying him for months, tried to play it down.

"Oh, nothing, " Apollo replied, "He was just talking about the bullying at school, because I hadn't told my grandparents about it up until now." Something inside of Apollo felt too ashamed to admit that he was the victim of even more bullying. He thought it made him look weak, and less of a man somehow. He decided to pull a fake yawn then.

"I'm tired," Apollo gestured sleepily, noticing it was now nearly four in the morning. "You can take my bed if you like, and I'll take the couch," Apollo offered, ever the gentleman.

Alora wasn't going anywhere though, without one last kiss. She kicked her heels off and leaned forward into Apollo as he lay back on the couch. This time their kiss was hot and passionate, filled with fire and urgency. They were both coming into their sexuality, ready to explore themselves and each other. Apollo suddenly felt himself becoming too aroused and was the first to pull back. Besides, he respected this girl too much to try anything. Instead, he cupped Alora's sweet face in his hands and looked down at her adoringly.

"Wow, you are such a vision, my Greek goddess; let me christen you Aphrodite, Goddess of Love, a beautiful deity whose angelic face could soften even the hardest of hearts."

CHAPTER TEN

Run for Your Life

In July of 1989, the school athletics carnival was on and Apollo had been training hard for it, religiously showing up for practice, determined to beat Gavin and Simon, who were considered the school favourites because they were the biggest and most developed of all the boys on the track. But Apollo's legs were sturdy and muscular, and while he was short he was very, very fast; so fast in fact, that his running coach had given him a nickname: The Bullet.

Alan and Mary were mostly absent since the altercation at home with Angela, and for all of Apollo's lack of friends and family dysfunction, things had now stabilised somewhat and life finally felt more routine, consistent. Troy was often found playing his video games or on the computer, oblivious to everything going on around him; he was a good kid at school, and while he wasn't a star student like Apollo, he never got himself in any trouble and was perfectly content with his life. Apollo, being the more sensitive, craved the stability of home life and could finally say he too was feeling more content with the current state of the world, all things considered. Of course the bullying remained a constant too, but Apollo now knew what to expect, because in his mind he had reduced Gavin, Simon and Cale to nothing more than slugs that wriggled around, trying to eat their way through apple cores; now, they had become insignificant to him because … well, they were just slugs.

But Alora was Apollo's rock and she was very much a prominent and strong constant in his life, despite the fact that he hadn't yet met her family; and her girlfriends and pretty much everyone else in her circle had no idea how close they had gotten. Yet the athletics carnival day had arrived, and Apollo knew Alora would be there to cheer him on. It would be a day they would never forget.

On a crisp Friday morning in July, Apollo sprang out of bed when usually he liked to sleep in; the day had arrived to show Gavin Croosy and his mates just what this little Greek boy was made of. It had been a long time coming, Apollo thought, and he was ready; his entire system was charged, and he was a wire of electricity, fired up and ready to win.

Yiayia made the boys a hearty breakfast of sfougato, a Greek frittata of eggs and vegetables with a side of tiganopsomo, a strong fried bread made of leavened dough, olive oil and salt, with a centre filling of feta and herbs.

"My boy will do well today. I can just feel it," Yiayia stated positively, ever the superstitious and wise one.

"Thanks, Yiayia," Apollo said, ravenously eating up his breakfast.

"This is good Greek fuel, it has served many men well in battle, and it'll serve you well today, too," she added, for extra sustenance. "Just do your best, Apollo—it is all you can ever do in this world," she winked proudly.

Apollo nodded quietly; Yiayia's undying support meant the world to him, and he was always grateful for her. He realised she had probably been up baking since dawn, too, and he admired her for her strength; the woman just never seemed to age.

When Apollo finally made it to the track it felt like the entire school was already there; his eyes searched for Alora, and he found her right away, sitting over by the benches with a group of girlfriends. He smiled and she waved, then came racing over to him. Alora was a knockout; she had woken up early and had showered and applied her make-up, paying extra attention to her hair and nails. She never wore makeup to school and didn't understand the girls that did. "What are they getting so dressed up for?" she'd once remarked. "It's not like it's anything special—it's like, school, duh—it's for learning." But today was special, and Alora made no secret of her affections either as she kissed Apollo in front of everyone and began rubbing his back. He felt like he was already king, and suddenly the race didn't even seem to matter, because this girl on his arm was finally his. Gavin and Simon happened to pass by just then, and noticed Alora patting his back.

"Oh, look at the loser and his little girlfriend—can't believe he even has the nerve to try out today," Croosy taunted and mocked.

"Haha, just watch the wog, he's gonna run dead last, wait and see!" Croosy's little sidekick, Simon added.

"Yeah right, " Apollo fired back, "Well, don't get ya girly knickers in a knot when I beat ya at the finish line! C'mon white bread, catch me if you can!" Apollo had to admit, for all the racial slurs he'd endured these past two years, he was finally dishing it back.

Even the word wog seemed to be losing its power and its sting now as though he were somehow now immune to it, having heard it so often.

Gavin turned and smirked, "Let me show you what a real winner does, hey, little Greek boy." Alora grew quiet then; the tension and rivalry was palpable, and deep down she worried for Apollo's safety.

The athletics carnival was now only an hour away; Apollo spent time stretching his muscles and limbering up and talking with his coach. He felt good—but even more importantly, he felt mentally positive and strong.

The sports presenters began announcing the carnival events in order, starting with the discus event, followed by javelin, and then the 4 x 100 metre relay race, ending the day with the biggest event: the cross country run.

The whole school had packed into the benches, and it was standing room only by the time it got to the cross country event. When Apollo took his place in the line-up amongst ten other boys who had been selected to compete, there were jeers from some of the kids in the crowd, kids who he'd figured were mostly friends with the bullies. He could hear them laughing at how little and short Apollo was compared to the other runners, certain he was going to finish dead last. Apollo mentally blocked out their taunts, looking instead for Alora in the crowd; he quickly found her sitting with a group of her girlfriends. She waved and smiled and Apollo felt a surge in his bones through her encouragement and suddenly there was a shift in his self-confidence, too, as it rose.

The sports presenters lifted their flags and blew their whistle as the race started, and away they went. Apollo, boosted by his sudden rise self-confidence, took off like the bullet that he was amidst a sea of legs all pounding the earth and blazing away; Gavin and Simon were sprinting at full pace, their long lanky legs making great strides and leading the way as the crowd cheered from a distance. The first hundred metres down the land was flat, and the runners sat close so early in the race. In the next section, Apollo focused on his speed and endurance as he came up upon hillier and undulating terrain. His track spikes gripped the green earth under him, kicking up dirt as he powered forward. He was in the zone and unaware of all space and time; only the words of his coach came to him now as he thought of all the training he had done up until this moment.

"Remember: don't come out too strong, you want to keep some reserve in the bank for the final stretch—just keep and hold pace, that's the only job you have to do; and stay under the radar and don't let loose until you're ready to pull the trigger on these boys."

Apollo kept pace; like the tortoise and the hare, he stayed steady and strong, the wind whipping him in the face. Surprised by his own speed and endurance, Apollo didn't just stay with the pack; he could feel himself growing stronger instead of weaker now with every passing stride. He crept quietly into fourth place, then into third. He could feel the strength of his core and how it had grown lean and muscular, adding to his already natural athleticism. The constant training had paid off—and now, with just two hundred metres to go, he knew it was going to be all down to him. He kept his eyes focused on Gavin and Simon just ahead; Gavin was leading the way, and Apollo was now nipping at Simon's heels. Simon saw Apollo coming up on the outside and he stuck out his elbow.

"Fucking wog," he wheezed breathlessly.

Apollo glanced sideways at Simon but said nothing; the surge inside of him was so great now, he seized the moment and overtook Libbs on the bend as his red face turned to a look of pure frustration.

Now Apollo was chasing down Croosy; and Gavin, not being able to see Apollo coming up from behind, had no idea how close the little Greek boy was gaining on him. Apollo was practically breathing down the big kid's shirt as the crowd rose to their feet and started going wild. Apollo could hear the chants echoing 'Croosy, Croosy,' but it was all just noise to him now. Croosy looked sidelong then and spied Apollo out of the corner of his eye, stunned as he was to see him right on his tail. But Apollo remained focused and clear-headed, he knew he could win this; his training had given him a new set of skills and he was wary of his opponent's space invading his space as they closed in on the last hundred metres. He knew that these two boys weren't going to go down without a fight, and Simon struggled to push his way back, gaining pace once again on Apollo. At the last turn and with just thirty metres to go they both attempted to cut Apollo off, giving each other a look of approval as they did. Unbeknownst to them, Apollo had predicted a similar fate, and as they both turned to take the corner coming side on, Apollo 'The Bullet' knew this was the moment, and he pulled the trigger, side stepping them both with great agility. He spun around them both as they lost their footing, falling over behind him. Apollo gleefully turned and pushed hard, full steam ahead, the wind hitting him in the face. I am the wind, he whispered to himself, thinking of his long-lost friend, Massimo, and thinking of Cyprus, his homeland. Ecstatic now, Apollo raised both arms above his head as he crossed the finish line first.

Croosy crossed second, the look of defeat all over his face. It was all the more embarrassing for the fact that up until that point he had dominated the entire race. Simon crossed into third place looking sheepish, given that he had thought their win was a sure thing. The crowd erupted in excitement and the sports presenters and teachers all stood there speechless. Alora was up on her feet cheering, so delighted for Apollo that she ran to him now, her hands flapping about excitedly in the air. He took her into his arms and they embraced.

"My God! You did it! You did it! You won!" She screamed like crazy. For the quiet and reserved girl who had only ever preferred reading and art galleries to sporting events, this was a whole new side of Alora he hadn't yet seen. Yet her pride for Apollo was genuine; it was written all over her face.

Apollo climbed onto the podium to receive a gold ribbon for first prize; Gavin and Simon entered the podium after him, their red faces flushed with anger as they shot Apollo spiteful looks. As Apollo passed by them, Gavin shouldered him, nudging him as he leaned in his ear and said, "We're gonna smash your motherfucking wog face in after school." Apollo knew they were infuriated that their perfect record of being top athletes at the carnival had now been broken and beaten by the likes of a much smaller and seemingly inferior opponent. Alora heard Croosy's threat and took it upon herself to fight back.

"Oh, grow up you two losers—he beat you fair and square and you know it," she said fearlessly. Croosy just looked at her and scoffed, seething with the word, "Later."

Apollo was touched that someone, anyone, would stand up and defend him, and he was moved by Alora's loyalty; but he was still a proud Greek, and he wouldn't allow a woman fight his battles for him.

"I've got this," Apollo said to her, still pumped by his win.

Right now he felt invincible; if he could have been an emperor, or leader of the free world in that moment he would have. Not sure whether it was him or the testosterone talking, he marched back over to Gavin and Simon, who were now leaning up by the chain link fence by the gate's exit. Yiayia and Frank would be coming any minute to pick up Alora and Apollo, yet Apollo felt it was his time; it was now or never. Croosy saw Apollo approaching them, and directed a menacing stare in his direction. Alora was quick to follow Apollo; as he came face to face with Croosy, Alora quickly placed her hand across Apollo's chest in an attempt to stop him.

"Don't worry, Alora, I got this," Apollo assured her again.

"But they're so much bigger than you—and you're just so tiny," Alora whispered tearfully.

Tiny. Ouch. That word cut through Apollo's ears just then, like a knife straight into his heart. The word tiny hurt even more than wog now. He couldn't believe what she'd just said, but he didn't have time to care, he was just too pumped up. Instead, Apollo looked back at Croosy and smiled. He could feel himself channeling his anger into something new, and it felt calm and controlled, the way a boat cuts effortlessly through the seas, shifting course, yet always on course and always steady, its big white sails guiding it gently forward.

Croosy came at Apollo then; he reached for Apollo's shirt as Apollo quickly raised his arm, deflecting him.

"You fucking little shit!" Croosy yelled, but Apollo was undeterred; the last two years of bullying had fuelled him on, and he deflected punch after punch that Croosy threw at him. Then it was Apollo's turn to attack; he stepped in, grabbing Gavin's wrist with such speed and precision that he turned his arm inside out, and with an open palm he whacked Gavin, striking him across the face with one mighty blow. Then came the second hit, again across the face and throat, winding Croosy as he fell to the ground, gasping for air. Apollo turned and faced Simon.

"Come on punk, come on you donkey, what are you waiting for? Let's go for it!" Apollo yelled, all jets firing. Simon looked at Apollo with shock then back at Gavin, who was on the ground struggling for air, and he bolted. Apollo turned and faced Alora, who was standing there, her jaw hanging open in disbelief.

"Oh my God—wow ... that did not just happen," she muttered, disbelievingly. "Wow, how did you do all that? I am so sorry I ever doubted you, Apollo. My God, you were amazing. My God, my God," she just kept repeating, stunned. She reached up and hugged Apollo with everything she had. The year had been such a disaster in so many ways, but in Apollo's mind this day had all but made up for it. Revenge was sweet, he reasoned, thinking of his favourite book, *The Count of Monte Cristo*. In the book, Edmund Dantès seeks revenge on his enemies, even though the priest he meets along the way warns him that to seek revenge is not good, and that he should channel his energies towards doing good. But there still came some small sense of payback and satisfaction for Apollo in that he had needed to level the playing field a bit after the years of bullying he'd endured at the hands of Croosy and his mates. Sometimes, a small amount of healthy revenge was ... necessary.

Apollo realised he needed to focus on his budding romance with Alora now, and it was as though something in him had been set free long enough to allow him to heal. The win had been a small feather in his cap, and he and Alora would proudly relay the events of the day to Yiayia and Papou that night over a special dinner. Alora and Apollo shared a kiss later that night, Alora wrapped in his arms.

"I really am looking forward to the day I get to meet your parents and family," Apollo said softly, looking deep into her azure blue eyes. He could get lost in those eyes, he thought, as blue, as deep and as mysterious as the Mediterranean sea. Alora looked back and smiled.

"Soon, my darling. Soon."

CHAPTER ELEVEN

Karate Kicks

Pumped by the success of his recent win, Apollo spoke to Yiayia about finally signing him up for karate, and Yiayia, thrilled that her grandson now wanted to venture into the sport, found the nearest karate dojo in Coburg, called Shotokan Karate. The classes ran on Monday and Wednesday nights, and Apollo was chomping at the bit, constantly asking Yiayia when it was going to start.

"Yiayia, I want to ask you a small favour," Apollo said as they rode along in the car together to his first lesson.

"Yes, my child, you can always ask me anything," Yiayia said, turning off Bell Street and onto busy Sydney Road in Coburg, looking for the number of the studio. Yiayia saw it first; however, they would have driven right by it, if not for the black banner displaying the word 'Karate' running vertically down the wall as it sat sandwiched between a funky '80s cafe on one side and The Deli, a rustic looking shop selling all manner of international cheeses and cold meats on the other. Yiayia immediately thought she could easily sit here and pass the time while she waited for Apollo to have his lesson as the store pumped festive international music out onto the street.

"Thank you for helping me get signed up for this, I really think karate is going to do great things for my self-esteem," Apollo confessed. "I just want to ask you not to tell anyone I'm doing this—I don't want anyone to know about it. It could make me more of a target."

"A target for what?" Yiayia asked, looking puzzled.

Apollo figured the time had come to tell Yiayia about Gavin Croosy, Simon Libb and Cale Moss and all the bullying he had faced on account of being short, and well, Greek.

Yiayia was visibly angry, but silently nodded, understanding him. She always understood everything. She just wished Apollo had been able to open up to her earlier; she wished he hadn't had to face all of this alone. She agreed that karate would do wonders for his self-confidence and overall development, so she promised to support him and not tell a soul. Apollo had been doing so well; he had kept up on taking his endocrine tablets from the hospital, as well as his six-monthly check-up appointments with Dr Stevenson, who had made several pleasing comments about Apollo's overall improvement.

Apollo climbed out of the car and entered the studio, leaving Yiayia to explore the deli; seeing the array of mats all over the floor, he looked around, wondering who he was supposed to meet.

The main instructor, John, came over to introduce himself. John was a round faced man with a smooth, bald head and friendly smile, and Apollo took an instant liking to him.

"Welcome to Shotokan Karate, Apollo! We are glad to have

you with us," John said in a husky voice. "We have sensei here who have a lifetime of karate experience, and with just a few months of training you will have some of the basic techniques that can be practiced and employed throughout your life. But it is a strict discipline, and the training is hard, so we expect you to be fully committed," he said, looking Apollo in the eye. Apollo nodded solidly without batting an eyelid.

"Good. Well, Shotokan style karate brings with it many great benefits, the most important being greater focus, increased self-esteem, increased self-discipline, calmness, and a more positive attitude towards life, as well as a knowledge of self-defence. The main focus of Shotokan karate training is the perfection of character—you are really here to challenge yourself by learning this strong but most beautiful art of Empty Hand. Are you ready to begin?"

"Yes!" Apollo was so excited he could have almost jumped out of his skin.

"Right—well, follow me this way, and we will get you set up first with your karategi; this is your karate uniform that you will wear to class. It is different from the judogi, which is a similar in look, but much heavier. So we will put on this white jacket first, the uwagi," he said, fitting Apollo with it, "then your canvas pants, which we call shitabaki, and lastly your belt, your obi. Your obi is different colours to indicate your ranking, or level of skill. Any questions so far?"

"Er, umm, I don't think so," Apollo replied nervously.

"Great—Okay, follow me over to the floor now for your first lesson and we will talk about Shotokan," John said, passing by some other people all dressed in white. One guy was particularly short, which Apollo liked, and he was wearing a black belt.

"That there's our Head Kata Coach, Max, he's a world champion black belt and our highest sensei here," John said proudly. "And that woman over there is Marina; she's twenty-two years of age and she has been training with us for two years, she's really good—and this guy on the end is Julian, our Tokaido champion."

Apollo felt truly humbled to be in their presence and felt the need to make a half bow as they passed by. *Wow,* he thought to himself. *If only the clowns at school could see me now!* John gestured for Apollo to take a seat on the floor mat. He would go on to explain that Shotokan style had developed from various martial arts by Gichin Funakoshi and his son, Gigō Funakoshi.

"But Shotokan is actually safer than Kyokushin karate, because the striking style has less power, while the Kyokushin style enforces harder strikes to knock out opponents."

That's what I want, Apollo thought; *I wanna knock 'em out.*

John continued, "But the truth is that Shotokan, although being the quieter brother to Kyokushin, actually employs even more destructive techniques—aimed at entirely destroying, maiming or even killing your opponent. For example, consider street fighting, or a life or death situation; mastering the Shotokan moves will get you out of any situation in a New York minute."

Yes, yes, this is good; keep talking, keep talking, Apollo thought to himself.

"In our lessons you will learn to master the basic techniques of sparring and self defence, which involves throwing, take-downs and reaping techniques, as well as kata, or patterns. Here, let me demonstrate some; I'll show you." John got up off the floor and assumed position. "This is called the zenkutsu-dashi, or front-forward leaning stance—not that any fight would have you starting at this point, because of course in reality that's ridiculous; in a real fight situation no-one has the time to line up their feet exactly so. This is more about getting you to think about your centre of gravity, how it allows you to brace yourself, find the most stable position on your feet, allowing for your weight to shift so your power can transition from lower body to upper body … like this." John shifted his weight from back leg to front leg, demonstrating the position. "It's really all about balance; and when you have already assumed the greater balance, you immediately have the upper hand."

Yes. Apollo thought about how Alan had thrown his head into the kitchen bench top, how he had been lower than him at the time, and how it was probably this, combined with a poor posture that had already sealed the deal, and made him weaker than his opponent, allowing him to be overpowered and overtaken.

"Now—think about all the karate you've ever seen on TV, like Bruce Lee, or Jackie Chan. They all use this one move, because it is simply the most powerful move in the world: the back kick. The back kick is so powerful, because it can generate the maximum amount of power in a short thrust, with the most force being delivered with the most depth, which is why it is called the back kick. Some call it the spinning back kick, or the turning back kick … whatever. The point is, when done by an expert, it can be very fast, too fast for your opponent to react."

Apollo fantasised about kicking Alan in the head just then, back when he'd had his head in a plastic bag that day. If only he'd known this back then, it could have saved him in so many situations.

"Now, let me show you what to do with your hands; they are very powerful weapons you know, and you must be very careful with them," John warned. "See here," he said, lowering his hands to well below his belt. "The hands here are positioned too low, exposing the upper body. And here, the entire groin is exposed to attack along with the lower body …"

Again, Apollo drifted off into his thoughts. Suddenly in his imagination, he could see himself in a back alleyway, facing off against Croosy in the dark of night. Croosy was trying to throw punches at various parts of Apollo's body, but with Apollo's new-found karate skills he deflected them all, one by one, catching Croosy by surprise and delivering the most spectacular, whip-snapping spinning back kick, compliments of yours truly. Apollo vs. Croosy, 1-0. It was awe-inspiring stuff, and Apollo shuddered in excitement. Already he was feeling stronger, just from listening to the sensei's wise words.

Apollo thanked John for the best first lesson ever and bounded down the staircase and out the door into the pelting rain, jumping for joy.

"Oh my God, Yiayia, it was awesome! I love karate! Thank you so, so much," he said, kissing her forehead and climbing in the passenger seat.

When Apollo returned to school he couldn't explain it, but something had happened. Whether it had been because he'd won the cross country meet, or if he was exuding some new Jackie Chan aura that frightened them all, but the bullying had finally stopped, more or less; at least for now on a physical level. Whatever the cause had been, the effect was immediate. Apollo's grades picked up again and he was more confident than ever, thanks to his karate. Not only that, but things with Alora were great, and they had become as close as two friends could get. Of course he loved Yiayia and Papou, but life was so much nicer because of his love for Alora and her connection with him. He felt truly blessed.

Midyear exams came and went, and school was improving; Apollo had been doing martial arts as a green belt for a while now, and with his speed and strength increasing, his self-confidence grew, and he was excelling not just at school, but in most things in life.

Troy and Apollo had come to accept the weird estrangement from their parents; they'd lost all contact with Mateus long ago, and now only learned about him through word of mouth and the Greek Cypriot community, which had a strong gossip grapevine. Apparently, he was still with the schemingly beautiful Olivia Bridges, and they had begun wedding preparations somewhere because Olivia now wanted to have children. *God help them,* Apollo thought, *if they bring more children into the world, only to treat them as poorly as they've treated their two sons.*

Mary and Alan had moved to the south end of Melbourne near Chadstone, and Apollo couldn't help feeling more than a little dejected and abandoned; but this only happened when he allowed himself to think about it, because the truth was that he couldn't bring himself to go there—it was just all too painful. It had been months and months since there'd been any word at all from Mary, and he felt completely unloved by his mother as a result. Yet Yiayia and Papou were always there to keep him in good spirits, and he loved nothing more than spending cosy nights at home with his grandparents and brother, enjoying a game of tavli; or he and Troy would hook up for a mad marathon session of *Double Dragon* and *Golden Axe,* two of their favourite video games.

Above all now, Alora was his world, and New Year's Eve 1989 would come to mark three years that they had known one another. Angela and Frank had decided to do something special, so they'd arranged to take both Apollo and Troy to a New Year's Eve function in North Coburg near the lake for a dinner dance and a mini disco nightclub afterwards. The night was a magical affair, and more exciting than in previous New Year's when they'd all just sat at home in front of the telly. Papou and Yiayia got all dressed up in their finest, Yiayia donning her favourite jewellery that she's salvaged and managed to bring with her from Cyprus; both the boys looked smart too, in white shirts and ties. The atmosphere was electric with great food and great music, and they dined the night away, looking forward to the disco and the countdown, which included spectacular fireworks to round out the evening. At ten minutes to midnight, Apollo grabbed Alora by the hand and led her outside by the lake, under the stars. He finally had to tell her how he felt about her.

"Alora; you mean the world to me. I wouldn't be becoming the man I am without you—you have supported me, and you have seen me through so much, and I just … I just … I have to tell you: I am in love with you." There. He'd said it. He looked to her now for a response, his eyes soft, hopeful.

"Apollo—you know I feel the same way," she said, holding back a tear. They shared a kiss and she pulled him in close and tight. "I just wish you were taller so I didn't have to bend down to kiss you all the time."

Apollo suddenly feeling sick, fell silent, and not knowing what to do or how to react, lowered his head in the moment to keep her from seeing his pain. His head felt confused, and he suddenly felt horribly embarrassed by Alora's words. How could she say such a thing? Wasn't love supposed to be blind? Weren't you supposed to love someone for who they were, not what? That was how Yiayia had raised Apollo, at any rate. He may have been a little short, he thought, but he was never short on morals or values. Alora pulled his face up by his chin; she had turned sixteen long before him and, sensing that something was off, said that she wanted him to meet her parents in the morning, that she wanted and was ready for more in their relationship.

"Okay," Apollo said, feeling doubly confused. It was a good thing that he was finally getting to meet her family after all this time, but there was now this niggling doubt in the back in his mind as to whether Alora could love him just for being him. Still, he thought it best to let the matter slide; it had been a nearly perfect New Year's Eve, and in the grand scheme of things Apollo had nothing really to complain about; things were going so well for him in every other area of his life that he just wanted to forget about it.

The next morning, on New Year's Day, Alora had her brother Paul pick them both up from Yiayia and Frank's house and bring them back to her family home in Northcote. Apollo was nervous as he hopped in the car; he greeted Paul, hoping her older brother would at least like him. Paul turned to greet them both from the driver's seat; he even smiled and shook Apollo's hand, a sign which Apollo saw as encouraging. As they started driving, Paul smirked cheekily, looking back in the rearview mirror.

"So, Alora—when did you start dating little boys much younger than you? What are you, Apollo? Ten or twelve? Ha ha."

Alora yelled at the top of her lungs. "Paul—oh my God, Paul! Why don't you shut up! Apollo is fifteen, and he's going to be sixteen ... Okay, smart arse?"

Apollo was more than a little humiliated that her brother would make such a comment, but he remained quiet as Alora cuddled him and took his hand in the backseat. Finally they arrived at the house. Con, Alora's father, who was sprawled out on the couch was a relatively big and burly man who worked hard as a builder. Alora's mother, also named Mary, worked part-time as a nurse in the pediatric unit at the local hospital. Mary was in the kitchen preparing an early lunch when Alora and Apollo arrived together.

"Mum, Dad—I'd like you to meet my boyfriend, Apollo," she said a little nervously. Con sized Apollo up and down, then offered his big panda hand up to Apollo for a handshake.

"G'day Apollo; well, you're not a bad-looking bloke! How old are you?" Apollo laughed and stammered, not sure if it was a compliment or not.

"I will be sixteen in the next couple of weeks, sir," he said, looking at his feet. Con and Paul both glanced at one another.

"Well, kori mou; it looks like you will be the one wearing the pants in this relationship," Con joked, and he and Paul both laughed. Alora rolled her eyes at her father and grabbed Apollo by the hand, dragging him off to safer quarters in the kitchen.

"Hi Mum, this is Apollo, and Apollo, this is my Mum, Mary."

"Mary? Wow—that's the same name as my mother," Apollo remarked, then winced at the mention of her name. What if Mary started to ask more questions about his mother? He just didn't want to go there.

"Nice to meet you, Apollo," Mary smiled warmly. "My, Alora—you certainly know how to find the cute ones," she smiled, winking at him. So, tell me about yourself, Apollo—may I ask though, you are in high school, yes? Sorry to ask, you are just so small and curious looking … how old are you?"

Apollo tried to hide his disappointment; his ears were still ringing from the car ride with Paul's derogatory comments which he still hadn't managed to digest or process. Now this? What were all the attacks on his height, all of a sudden? Apollo grew nervous;

he hadn't imagined it ever going like this, or being this hard. He took a deep breath and swallowed hard.

"I will be sixteen in two weeks, Mary," he said, trying to keep his voice steady.

"Sixteen. Wow," was all she could say in reply. Awkward pause.

"In two weeks," Alora added, for extra measure. Alora's mother was quiet for a moment.

"Hmmm. Okay, well then let's all sit down to eat—lunch is ready," she said, arching her body around the corner to get her husband's attention. "Come on you two," she called out to her son and everyone came to sit down to eat.

There were no more questions asked during lunch; the family shared their Greek family history with Apollo; originally they'd hailed from Sparta, and they feasted on Greek food they swapped stories about their families. Apollo could finally feel himself relaxing back into himself as his embarrassment subsided. Lunch went well, yet Apollo still couldn't shake his disappointment. He was on a downer; his confidence had been shattered with the cutting comments about his height and he felt he was always an easy target, even though he had always tried his best to roll with life's punches.

No: I am a new person, he thought to himself. I am a confident person now. I am a cross country runner. I am a winner. I am a karate freak. I am a karate-Do; I am a Karateka 空手家! Apollo knew that, depending on how he felt on any given day, he could be super confident or he could be on a complete downer, and right now he felt as though he were on a tightrope, trying ever so delicately to maintain his balance between staying in control and flipping out. Apollo was working so damn hard at just trying to hold it all together that it was exhausting him.

"Okay, who wants some Vasilopita, eh?" Mary said, cutting into the cake. She cut a slice for Christ and placed it in the centre first, then began passing out slices around the table, from oldest to youngest.

"Who's going to get the coin? I wonder," Paul asked excitedly.

"Because you weren't here last night and were out galavanting with this boy," Con started, glancing at Apollo, "we have left the presents from Saint Basil, to celebrate Protochronia, for you in the living room to open later."

"Okay, thank you, Papa," Alora said, suddenly feeling guilty for having not been home on New Year's Eve. She knew it was her family's favourite celebration besides Easter, and she was suddenly sorry that she'd ruined it.

Alora's mother Mary found the coin in her cake. "Lucky me—about time I got this coin, I can feel my luck about to change right now, because Paul is going to get up and offer to do the dishes!" she laughed, in response to Paul's monkey face groans.

Apollo was relieved when he heard Alora announce that they were leaving, because for him, this had been more than enough for one day. Apollo wished them all a happy New Year, proud of himself just for keeping it all together. Just as they were about to head out the door, Alora's father, Con, couldn't resist taking one more jab at Apollo.

"Hey, Alora—careful you don't get pregnant with your boyfriend, Alora mou! You don't want to be raising midgets!" Alora quietly shut the door behind her, but Apollo could still hear them all laughing inside long after they'd gone.

Ouch.

Once they were outside, Alora grabbed Apollo by the arm. "Goddamnit! Why did my family have to go and ruin everything?

I am so sorry, babe; he is just joking—seriously—he is just joking. Just ignore him, okay, babe? Please? For me?"

But Alora saw the look of pain in Apollo's eyes, and it was the pain of a thousand years past and a thousand years being carried forward for a thousand years more. There was so much transference of pain in the history of the world, in the history of time; pain even lay in the wreckage of Cyprus, it was in the remnants, in and amongst the ruins. Pain would be there, because pain would always be there, and that's just how it was.

CHAPTER TWELVE

Sixteen Candles

Two weeks later, Apollo was blowing out the candles on his birthday cake and celebrating his sixteenth birthday with Alora by his side.

"Make a wish, Apollo," Yiayia said, ever superstitious about life.

"God give me justice," he whispered into thin air, barely audible. But Alora heard him; not clearly, but enough to understand.

"Did you know that the blowing out of candles on a cake is rooted in ancient Greek history?" Yiayia wanted them to know. Troy rolled his eyes.

"Oh no, not all that Greek history stuff again," he said, snorting at his grandmother. "That was so long ago, and it doesn't matter now because we live here, in the present," he said, matter-of-factly. Troy was the complete opposite of Apollo and about as far from being a sentimentalist as any modern-day kid could get.

"This generation has no respect for history, for the past—"

Papou grumbled, "but if it wasn't for the past, you wouldn't BE here!" he wheezed, which sent him coughing and spluttering into a full-blown asthma attack.

"Whatever," Troy said, stuffing birthday cake in his mouth.

"I like history," Apollo said quickly. "Please continue, Yiayia, I want to know," he said, shooting Troy an angry look. He knew how much history meant to Yiayia and could see that right now his brother was being nothing more than a X-Gen brat.

"Well," Yiayia continued, "it was an ancient Greek ritual to honour the goddess Artemis, who was associated with childbirth, wildlife ... and the moon. They started making cakes that were modelled after the moon as a tribute to Artemis, goddess of the moon. The cakes were made as circles, replicating the moon, then it was covered in candles to make it shine like the moon, too. And that's the story of why we have candles on birthday cakes," she said. "But I won't bore you with any more of my old lady talk."

"Thank you Yiayia; you know I always love your stories, and you are never boring," Apollo said, giving her a hug and shooting Troy another look. He could be so insensitive sometimes, just like their mother. And Apollo really did love Yiayia's stories, and they filled him with light and wonder of far-off places, transporting him to unseen lands in unseen times. It was a far more pleasant place to be, he thought, than being stuck in this place called reality.

Apollo felt a sudden pang in his heart then; it was his birthday, yet his birth mother, this woman who had brought him into the world, was nowhere to be seen. Mary and Alan had gone off to a new life together, and he felt he was just a forgotten piece of rubble left in the ruins. He couldn't deny it: it hurt like hell. How lovely it would have been to see his father Mateus again, to have both his parents here, celebrating his birthday; life had dealt him a cruel blow, and he didn't mean to sound ungrateful for all that Yiayia and Papou had given him. It was just that he felt that there was still something missing, and it felt like a hole in his heart. What had happened to that little boy who so long ago had looked out his window on a balmy Cyprus eve, knowing he would never see his home again? What had happened to his family that had once been intact, united? The sadness enveloped him and overwhelmed him then, and finally Apollo couldn't contain it any longer, and he buried his head in his hands.

Yiayia rushed to him. "Please, please don't cry my son, not on your special day," she said, stroking his hair and soothing him.

"It's okay, Yiayia, I'm okay. Really. Besides, this isn't really my special day anyway, it's September 3rd, remember? My name day."

"That's true," Yiayia nodded. "Today everyone celebrates his birthdays, but, if you asked any grandparent or old-timer like me when my birthday was or how old I am, most of us haven't the faintest idea—because back in those days it was only our name day that mattered. The world is changing, I guess," she sighed.

"Let's go, I'm taking you on a walk," Alora said suddenly, pulling Apollo out of his chair.

Alora and Apollo walked the suburban streets past the red brick houses lined with neat little gardens, counting the cracks in the sidewalk. Arm in arm they walked, matching their feet and coordinating their steps to mirror the other and walk in time. They were always playing silly, goofy games like that, and they laughed at the silliness of it. They kept walking together, down past the basketball stadium and following the creek all the way along that led to the lake reserve.

Alora went first down the embankment, and Apollo followed

her to a grassy knoll resting right by the edge of the lake. It was warm in the late afternoon sun, the rays dancing prettily at the water's edge, like silvery ballerinas spinning just on the surface of the water.

"It's pretty here, huh?" Apollo said as they sat, he playing with her hair in the sunshine.

"So pretty! There's no lake where I live in Northcote—it's too urban," Alora said, tilting her head back, allowing the sun's rays to caress her face.

"So, did you have a good birthday? Did you like your present?" Alora asked playfully. She had hunted down and found a first edition of *The Count of Monte Cristo* for Apollo; the look of surprise on his face when he opened the birthday wrapping had all been worth it.

"Oh my God! I love it! It's my favourite book. You shouldn't have," Apollo gushed. This girl was so thoughtful and so perfect for him in every way.

Alora was in the mood for a chat with Apollo; a serious chat. She turned into him, and they sat, kneecap to kneecap facing each other.

"Sooooo—Apollo, what I want to know is, what do you want to do with your life? I mean, once we finish school, babe; that's what I mean."

"Well I have been thinking about it a bit—" he ventured. "I have a couple of dreams; I would love to work with people, be it nursing or in the medical field. I feel like I have a calling to help people. And I kinda like older people, don't ask me why. Maybe I'm an old soul, or something," he shrugged. "What about you? What were you thinking of doing?"

"I always wanted to get into dancing, but also I wanted to

become a doctor or a midwife, you know, like work in hospitals and help people 'n stuff ..."

"No way! Really?"

"Yes, way," Alora replied, grinning. "Okay, well let's make a pact—we'll both work together to get to our dreams and follow them," Alora said, crossing her heart with her fingers and offering her pinkie up to Apollo in promise, to seal the pact. They linked fingers and Alora pulled Apollo in with her pinkie for a kiss. She was ecstatic that Apollo had similar dreams to her; they were just two peas in a pod, similar in so many ways. What started as a light kiss evolved into something deeper and more intense, and Apollo had to pull back because it was all getting too hot and steamy, and his emotions were flying.

"I promised my parents, especially my mother, that I would wait till marriage before sex," Alora said softly, and Apollo respectfully nodded.

"I understand, and I know that, coming from a Greek culture. I know from Yiayia that the old-school villages were brought up respectfully in the Greek church. And we have to honour that tradition," he said, kicking at the tufts of grass by the edge of the lake.

"Hey, I'm suddenly ravenous!" Alora said, jumping to her feet. "Wanna go get a slice of Newland's pizza with me?" She said, pulling him up off the grass. Apollo stumbled to his feet and together they walked arm in arm, following the creek all the way back the way they'd came. Apollo was grateful for the distraction; he knew they were both coming into their sexuality now, and the kissing by the lake had been temptation enough—he knew he had to honour this girl, and he cared for her as though she were some rare, lost treasure that only he'd been lucky enough to find.

School wasn't starting back until the end of January and so

they would spend their holidays together, Alora always wanting more privacy with Apollo, but as a more reserved good girl she still wanted to take it slow. Apollo knew they were both virgins and that Alora wanted to take it to the next level; they could never get enough of each other, or enough time together alone, which in hindsight he realised was a good thing. Her parents were strict and she'd wanted to honour their wishes, so there would be no sex before marriage, which Apollo knew was going to be hard.

"I just didn't plan on falling in love at such a young age," she said, pulling Apollo into a kiss. "I am in love with you, my gorgeous little Greek boy," she said, looking up into his eyes as they prepared to say goodnight. Apollo loved hearing her speak these words and told her the same.

"I love you too, gorgeous." He kissed her and they went their separate ways, looking forward to the new year together, and all it would bring.

***

1989 was upon them, and the beginnings of a new year beckoned; Apollo was now sixteen, yet he was still a very underdeveloped kid for his age. He was excelling in all his classes, and for the most part all the bullying was now a thing of the past, aside from the occasional snide comments that were directed towards him from time to time.

Apollo continued with his karate and things were going reasonably well. He had moved up from a green belt, channeling his anger into his training and watching his diet, and he knew he couldn't ruin it by backsliding into depression by revisiting painful things of the past. Instead, with the help of his dojo and sensei, he now took solace in the fact that he was just like any other normal teenager and simply needed a little more time to develop and adjust. To him, it was no longer a matter of wondering why the kids at school hated him and gave him a hard time; now he understood that it was only about liking himself, and this empowered him, unlocking the keys to who he was and what he could really be.

In five short months, Apollo had climbed the ranks at Shotokan Karate, advancing to his third belt and going from white to yellow to orange. Alora came to watch his gradings, and she was duly impressed. Today, Apollo would train with the Kata Head Coach, Max. Max was by far the most senior sensei at the Academy, and Apollo thought he was the best, too. For all his short stature, Max packed a punch, and he was spiritually attuned and devoted to his art.

"You see, karate is an art of peace—and you get to decide what you want to make out of it," he said as he and Apollo stretched and limbered up on the floormats. Alora sat off to one side watching them.

"Even the 'Ka' part of Shotokan means to gain—and maintain—mental balance and tranquility. One must learn and repeat all the aspects of Shotokan until they are perfect; only then does one become a true Karateka."

Apollo nodded and pulled at his obi belt to tighten it before they began just as sensei, too, adjusted his coveted black belt. On their separate mats they each assumed the zenkutsu-dashi forward facing position, which signified the beginning of every session.

"Right. So when you greet your sensei, or any black belt, you must always use two hands to show trust and humility, and then you say 'Osu' as a sign of respect."

"Osu," Apollo repeated, bowing to his new master.

"Karate is special, because it offers something that ironically most other sports do not do: it teaches one how to become less violent. It is proven that more fights in the dojo leads to less fights in the streets—and if you don't believe me, then let me prove it to you.

"The experience of controlled violence as both an attacker and defender and in a controlled and regulated setting like we have here allows us the opportunity for learning how to deal with violence. We can retrain our minds and how we react to certain situations—and those who practice Shotokan regularly become calmer even when they are provoked or bullied. Even when another student hits them they are able to maintain their cool and not let the situation slip out of their hands. Where just one year ago, they would go ballistic, we now see students practising all that we teach them, and they now have the tools they need to become less, instead of more, violent in tense situations. Indeed, they have learned the life skills that enable them to deal effectively with the demands and challenges of everyday life—which aggressive and violent people lack most of the time."

Apollo listened carefully to sensei's wisdom; he thought about how out of control Croosy had been, throwing punches at him; the volatile and crazed look in Alan's eyes that day in the kitchen, as though he were possessed. The sensei continued.

"We learn then, not to fight with anger, but with understanding. I see so many people come in here because they want to learn how to fight, or fight back—but it's because they feel weak out there, on the outside—when what they really need to learn is how they can start to feel strong on the inside, and compassionate on the outside."

Apollo nodded; even he had realised in his short few months here that his anger and fantasies of wanting to hurt Alan or Croosy had abated; he thought again about his favourite book, *The Count of Monte Cristo,* and how Edmund Dantès hunts down his enemies, seeking revenge upon them for all the horrible things they did to him. Yet Apollo could almost feel the anger draining from his body now, and in its place, came the arrival of peace, contentment, and respect for all living things.

"You must understand that karate is serious, and we learn this art, not to have an extra power or skill that we can lord over others to hurt them, like, say as a bully would do, but to strengthen ourselves, to seek perfection of character. In fact, revenge is the last thing karate must be used for; we must all take an oath that what we learn in here will not be used for violence of any kind, and this is called the Dojo Kun—an oath which states that you will never use karate for violence or for ill. One must promise a rule of no first attack; you must protect the way of truth; you must refrain from hot-blooded behaviour, to guard yourself against impetuous courage; and finally you must foster the spirit of effort, respect and etiquette."

"Yes, Sensei," Apollo whispered quietly, bowing his head.

"I have taught you many moves in these past months, and I think you are doing very well remembering them because now you have reached your orange obi; so for today we are going to focus on the mind," Sensei said, directing Apollo to the floor. "Then we will do some short role play with you as the Umi, or defender, while I will be the Tori, or attacker—then we will switch positions. This will give you some interesting insight, Apollo, because the Karateka cannot avoid the situation—thus, he or she has to learn to deal with it. Through this pattern of role-play you will learn how to deal with and experience both roles: being an attacker and being a defender. Sound good?"

"Yes, Sensei," Apollo nodded obediently.

"Remember: the ultimate goal of Shotokan karate is not winning or losing—but perfecting the character of who practices it."

"Yes, Sensei."

"Now, about our minds; they are tricky creatures, and we need to get control over them, because when we get control over the body and the mind, it leads us to more peaceful subjects. Right?"

"Right."

"For example, when somebody does us wrong, we can allow those thoughts of anger to consume us, control us. We pour all our energies into seeking revenge, being angry and feeling the injustice of the situation. With what I am going to teach you, you will be able to gain control over the mind—because control is the prerequisite for a happy and fulfilled life. When the mind affects our impulses, and negative emotions dominate our decision making processes, we can become clouded in our thinking, or fixated on seeking revenge or retribution. The further down this path we go, the less likely we are to reach happiness. But, when we master control of our mind, this leads us towards becoming more selfless, compassionate personalities that do not seek violence. Once we reach control over our body and mind, tranquility, balance, and resilience emerge. Opponents can become friends. Conflicts can become opportunities of mutual understanding. Jealousy changes into sympathy. And when we do all these things, we reach higher and higher levels of self-actualisation, getting ever closer to the perfection of character we ultimately seek. In fact, by losing our tendency towards toughness, Karate brings us closer than anything else to experiencing life as it was always supposed to be: peaceful. Can you feel the peace visiting with us now as we speak?" Sensei asked.

"Yes, yes, I can," Apollo answered quietly.

"Good. I think you are starting to demonstrate early mastery over your mind."

Sensei and Apollo would finish the session off with the role-play as Sensei had promised they would do. In previous lessons, Apollo had enjoyed the physicality of learning different moves like back kicks, throwings and take-downs; but this was different, and he knew it. Things were not yet fully clear to him, but things were definitely changing, and this was good.

"I love you, Apollo, and I'm so proud of you," Alora said, hugging Apollo after the session was over.

"I love you too, baby."

CHAPTER THIRTEEN

Oh, Baby

The year flew by and Apollo sailed through, achieving class honours for his efforts. Troy was also doing well at school and was involved in playing football for the local team while Apollo continued to advance in his karate. Life felt pretty routine and good and stable, and Gavin Croosy, Simon Libb and Cale Moss were too busy trying to get passing grades now to bother with Apollo.

One afternoon, Apollo left school early to come home because it was Tuesday 13th, and Yiayia, like most Greeks, had a real superstition about the date being bad. Apollo also wanted to come early and care for Papou; he hadn't been well of late, and the doctors had had him on medications after coming down with a severe bout of bronchitis. He was just about to make his Papou a hot cup of tsai tou vounou, a Greek mountain herbal remedy with iron wart that grew in the wild and hilly region of the Troodos mountains in Cyprus, when he heard the front door open.

"He is drinking plenty of visinada for its vitamin C content as well," Yiayia was saying, when she dropped the loaf of bread she'd been carrying mid speech as her eyes followed Apollo's gaze and laid eyes on who else but Mary as she stood in the doorway looking at them all.

"Oh, my!" Yiayia yelled, rushing to her daughter.

Apollo hadn't seen or heard from his mother in over eleven months; that day she had suddenly decided to call in and visit with Alan, bringing their new little bundle of joy with them in the form of a baby girl, which shook Apollo to his very foundations. *She still looks pretty much the same, perhaps overdoing it on the make-up,* Apollo thought. Maybe she didn't like the onset of new wrinkles forming at the creases of her eyes, or the wisps of grey now appearing by her ears. He also hadn't seen Alan in so long that he hardly recognised him; Alan had now grown a beard and bought a Harley Davidson. Probably the result of midlife crisis, Apollo chuckled to himself.

"This is your new little sister, Maggie," Mary announced proudly. "Everyone come and say hi," she said, rocking Maggie in her arms. Apollo and Troy were instantly smitten; then Alora, who had been sitting with Frank in the lounge room, came in the kitchen, and Frank and Angela both gasped with delight, wowed by Maggie's beauty. They all fussed over her, adoring this most precious new baby with ten perfect fingers and toes. But Frank and Angela couldn't help being very hurt and somewhat heartbroken, however, by the fact that they'd known nothing of the impending birth, not to mention how Mary had seemingly traded one family for another so suddenly, leaving her boys alone and without a mother or father in their lives. Yet now it seemed she was coming in to show off her new family and new life as though she had done nothing wrong.

"You have missed so much of what's been going on," Yiayia stated abruptly, scuttling in her slippers over behind Apollo, who'd had to sit down in all the commotion as he tried to process it all.

"Apollo here is becoming a karate master," Yiayia bragged, "… and Troy here is playing football—and they are both excellent students at school, too." Apollo knew his Yiayia meant well, but something inside him still angered and simmered just beneath the surface; he felt she didn't have a right to know anything about him, because in all the time she'd been gone she'd never even bothered or made any effort to find out about them. Still, he tried to remember his sensei's words now, and the training he was doing on learning to control his mind. Apollo was trying; Lord knew he was trying. It just wasn't working. Plus, he was frustrated because Yiayia had completely forgotten her promise to him to never tell a soul about his karate.

Apollo looked now at Mary; this was his mother, but he could barely say the word. He felt like he hardly knew her; who she was, or anything about her. His childhood with her now felt like nothing more than a sad, distant memory. He had become used to his absent mother and absent father, so he was in many ways happy to meet his little sister, as were Troy and Alora.

"Can I have a hold of her?" Alora asked politely, feeling clucky and maternal. She loved all children.

"Are you still seeing my son, Apollo?" Mary asked, but Alora did not dignify Mary's question with an answer, choosing instead to hand the baby back to her. Then she grabbed Apollo by the hand and dragged him off to the bedroom, closing the door to speak to him. Alora was growing into a very strong-willed and strong-minded girl who took charge of things, compared to the more passive Apollo, who was content with coasting along; yet in many ways they were still more similar than not. Apollo sensed that Alora wished he were more assertive, because she knew what she wanted and how to get it.

"She's a beautiful baby," Alora began, as they got comfortable on Apollo's bed and turned on the TV.

"Yes," was all Apollo could reply; his head was still spinning, still trying to process his mother's surprise visit. He was glad they were now tucked away in the safety of his bedroom though, because he really had no desire to see her. They sat like that for a few minutes, watching the evening news; then Alora grabbed the remote and, snatching it off him, turned the whole thing off. Instead, she grabbed his face by the jaw and pulled him closer into her; as she gazed into his eyes, they shared another kiss and things quickly became passionate. Then she pulled back.

"It's so hard waiting, Apollo," she moaned, feeling ready to take their relationship to the next level. "I do love and appreciate the fact that you are prepared to wait for me, though; your patience is both impressive and honourable." They lay together in the stillness and quietness like that for a while, wrapped in each other's arms. Apollo inhaled the intoxicating smell of Alora's hair, the scent of her, as she nuzzled into him. It drove him crazy. He was becoming more of a man now too, and the early signs of his facial hair coming in pleased him, because up until now his developmental delays had left him looking more like a boy than a man. His Adam's apple appeared, and his voice dropped an octave, and Alora found these new changes sexy in him.

That night, Alora went home as she had been staying over at Apollo's house more nights than not, even though he was always happy to take the couch and offer up his bed to her; but tonight,

Alora decided she needed to remove the temptation altogether and stay home for a while. They ventured out of Apollo's bedroom well after dark, and well after the circus of his mother, Alan, and the baby had left.

"Apollo, you did not come out to see your mother—it would have been nice," Yiayia said in an attempt to bridge past hurts. But Apollo had nothing to say; he just shrugged and went to the kitchen, helping himself to cold leftovers in the fridge and then proceeded to squeeze the death out of a lemon. His mother knew nothing about his life now, and he had begun to prefer it that way; she'd never known about the bullying, or the developmental delays he'd battled with; she was never there to see his track meets, or see his big cross country win; she knew nothing about his academic performance, or his finally making the honour roll, or his karate sessions or his relationship with Alora—heck, she hadn't even been at his recent birthday party! So what did he care? What he'd really wanted to say to Yiayia right then was that it would have been nice if his mother had shown even the tiniest millisecond of interest in his life in the past year, but he didn't dare.

"Did Alora leave? And so soon? I hope you two didn't have a fight …"

"Nope—all good. Night Yiayia, night Papou," Apollo said, kissing them both on the cheek.

The next day Apollo trudged off to school. He'd had to do some quick thinking with the maths teacher because he hadn't done his assignment; he'd been so thrown off his game by the sudden cameo appearance of Mary and Alan the night before. Alora didn't meet him at their usual lunch spot under the ancient liquid amber the next day, either, making the excuse that she was too far behind in her schoolwork and needed to go to the library and study.

"I'll come study with you, or I can help you if you like," Apollo offered. But Alora just shook her head and disappeared into the swarm of students mingling in the halls.

That night at home, Alora also had to face a barrage of questions about Apollo.

"He's a nice enough young boy," her father would say, "a great boy—but he is not the man for you, kori mou," he said, shaking his head.

"He's far too sensitive and way too underdeveloped," her mother added, "and you are too young to be getting serious like this; you have your whole life ahead of you."

"But I love him!" Alora would protest, although her pleas fell on deaf ears.

But her brother continued to stir her constantly, while her mother, though disappointed, kept quiet; she knew her daughter was hurting, but still felt she was staying with Apollo for the wrong reasons. Alora was struggling; she wanted her father's respect and approval, and she had to admit that even her older brother's thoughts and opinions mattered a great deal to her—more than she was willing to admit. Greek families, she concluded, had a lot of pull when it came to the outside world. She didn't quite understand why that was, but she had to just go along with it and accept it as fact. That was just how it was.

As the year went on, Alora began to change towards Apollo; she went days without seeing him or calling him, and even avoided him at school. Sadly, behind the scenes, her father's remarks and her brother's digs had taken their toll, swaying her to have doubts about her relationship. Apollo's stature and character were too sensitive; he was way too underdeveloped; they were both too young, and she was coming into the early stages of womanhood while he was still light-years behind her, developmentally. Even her girlfriends had gotten to her.

"What are you doing, why are you still with him—c'mon, you can do waaay better; he's a midget and he's punching well above his weight! Look at you, you're gorgeous, pussycat!" Tracy said, shaking her head in disbelief. All the girls started purring and meowing jokingly at Alora. Alora just rolled her eyes, thinking they were being ridiculous. Even chubby Amanda, who had by now slimmed down considerably at sixteen, had little positive to say about Apollo.

"He's too Greek, too short, too meek, too boring for you," she sneered.

"That's rich, coming from you, Miss Chubby Pants!" Alora shot back. "You know, you lot are starting to sound more than a little racist!"

But the majority of the girls Alora was friends with were Aussie girls who could only see Apollo for his nationality—which was different to theirs—therefore in their eyes he was just a 'wog' and would always be a wog, because to them he could never be anything else.

***

Alora knew in August of 1989 that she needed to have a conversation with Apollo about where this was all going because, at some level, she also knew that if she didn't broach the subject, he never would. She had noticed this too between her parents; on the odd occasion when they'd had to have a hard conversation, Con would always turn the other way, looking as though he'd been backed into a corner, while her mother had assumed the role of Miss Maturity and Responsibility as head matriarch of the family.

Alora had to wonder if it was just a Greek thing, that Greek boys tended to remain boys longer (or all their lives) because of the tight-knit mama-boy relationships they had with their mothers; or whether it was just because girls on average always matured faster than boys as a matter of biological fact. Perhaps it a combination of both, or all of the above; she just didn't know.

Whatever the case, Alora sensed Apollo's resistance the moment she suggested to him that they have a conversation. Perhaps he could sense that whatever was coming their way couldn't be good, based on the seriousness of her tone and the manner in which she had announced it. Irrespective of this, he reluctantly agreed to meet her under the darling liquid amber on the school grounds after school that Friday afternoon.

"Hey," Alora said, seeing Apollo approach, hands in pockets, body posture slumped forward.

The grass under the tree was green and lush from the hard winter rains, and as Apollo sat down he thought it smelled fresh and fragrant, just like his old home in Cyprus. Alora sat down beside Apollo on the downward slope of the hill, the fragrant smells of eucalyptus and gum and torn tree bark in the wind. Winter was on its way out, and the early buds of springtime were visible everywhere.

"Hey," Apollo replied, kissing Alora on the cheek. "I brought you something," he said, reaching into his pocket. He pulled out a red and white string bracelet he'd made himself by twisting the strings together, and he placed it around her wrist, tying it securely.

"What is it?" Alora asked, baffled.

"But you're Greek! You seriously don't know?"

"No."

"It's called a Marti bracelet—it's an ancient Greek tradition to symbolise the beginning of spring. You tie it around your loved one's wrist to wish them peace, purity, passion and life. Yiayia taught me."

"Oh."

"Well, normally it's given to wear March 1st to 31st; but since our seasons here are all upside down I'm giving it to you now …"

"Okay, well thanks, Apollo … that's very … umm … nice of you," Alora said, feeling like shit. "Look, Apollo, we have to talk. I know we haven't seen much of each other these past few weeks, and I'm to blame for this …" Alora said, trailing off. This was going to be hard, because she truly did love him, which was why she was having such a hard time finding the right words. Apollo, ever the gentleman, tried to help.

"I figured that since the New Year's lunch with your folks, they might be in your ear a bit," Apollo said sympathetically. Alora just sat there quietly nodding.

"It's true, they're not really in support of our relationship—"

"Well it's not really up to them, 'cos I'm not dating them, I'm dating you," he tried to remind her gently.

"I know, I know what you're saying," Alora agreed, edging away from him slightly, "but I think there are some reasons for us not to see each other right now … well, for right now, anyway …"

"Such as?"

"Well, for one thing, my parents … and then we have a lot of study pressures right now, Apollo. Look, don't make this harder than it already is—I just can't be with you right now … I need to do other things … and then there's our age difference … I'm nearly seventeen, and in three years I'll be wanting to marry, babies, all of those things—and look at you: you're only sixteen, there's no way you're ready for that if you can be truthful about it."

Apollo sat there feeling shattered, crushed, and heartbroken. He couldn't believe what he was hearing. He couldn't believe what she was uttering. His heart sank a million miles below sea level. Then he broke down right in front of her as she watched on, feeling absolutely devastated as well. Yet the truth was that not everyone approved of their being together, and Greek communities held a lot of power and weight over such things. They were trapped in this thing, as though stuck between the old world and a new world that had not yet made enough space for them to fit into it. Alora felt somewhat ashamed of what she was doing to Apollo right now because he didn't deserve it and because she knew he'd been through too much already. She went to speak again, to say something to console him, but instead he just got up.

"I have to go," he whispered, and walked away. And just like that, it was over. Alora looked down at her red and white Marti bracelet, then pulled her knees into her chest and howled.

Apollo went home, falling into a heap of depression, not knowing where to turn. But if he thought he'd been down before, that was nothing compared to this.

CHAPTER FOURTEEN

Where the Wind Blows

Apollo sobbed into his pillow for the better part of the weekend, thinking he'd be better off dead than having to live without his beloved Alora. He thought about how difficult it was to notice who wasn't there, and what wasn't there anymore; when he thought about Cyprus now, all he could see were birdless trees and treeless winds and strangers he'd never met, all walking around on cobbled lanes carrying his Cyprus heart without him. He wished more than anything to return to Cyprus where he belonged; because without Alora in his arms, there was nothing else keeping him here.

Troy could see his brother was suffering and went to him the next morning.

"C'mon, Bro," Troy said, trying to coax Apollo out of the doldrums. "We're the kings of Limassol, remember?"

Apollo offered up a faint half smile for his brother, appreciating the sentiment, but really he just felt empty inside. At the mention of Limassol, Apollo could see them then; he could see himself, Troy and Massimo as little boys playing down by the water's edge at the beaches in Cyprus. How they'd stood and posed together in matching swimsuits, waiting for a photograph together, arm in arm, while their mother had fumbled about with the camera. He buried his head under the pillow and told Troy to go away.

Yiayia, too, had tried various methods of getting Apollo up and out of bed, even inventing reasons as to why she needed him to get up.

"Your Papou needs help in the vegetable patch," she'd come and say. Two hours later she'd make up something else, like, "I've done something wrong to the video player and only you know how to get it working again!" being the adorable, well-meaning nuisance she could sometimes be. But Apollo wouldn't budge. He lay in bed like a bear with a sore head and ate soup, watched TV, and slept the days away. On Sunday night Yiayia brought in his favourite meal on a TV tray, her homemade lasagne.

"You're going to have to talk to me, Apollo—and you have school tomorrow, which you cannot miss, so you can't keep avoiding things forever," she said gently. He pulled his head out from under the covers and dared to show his face. His skin was blotchy, his eyes red and swollen, his hair a mess. His face was lifeless, expressionless, as though someone had just come along and erased an entire canvas. He felt defeated.

"I love her," was all he could bring himself to say.

"I know, I know, my son," Yiayia said, her heart aching for him. "Let me tell you a story—you'll like that. You say you like my stories, right?"

Apollo sighed. He sat up in bed and nodded.

"Well," Yiayia began, "There is an old story in Cyprus that dates back, ooh, I think to maybe the Middle Ages … anyway, it was about a beautiful girl, Cassandra, who was daughter to the last king of Troy. He had other daughters too, but Cassandra was by far the loveliest. Well, soon one of the Gods, Apollo, your namesake, fell in love with the stunning Cassandra. He just had to have her, so he decided to make her a proposition: if she agreed to marry him, he would give her the power of prophecy, of fortune telling—the ability to foresee everything before it came to be. She agreed, accepting the proposal and the gift. Apollo was quite happy with all of this because he finally thought he had won the woman of his dreams! Or so he thought …"

Yiayia now had Apollo's full attention. He looked at her, wide-eyed, wondering where this was leading.

"So anyway, Apollo gives her the gift, but then when he goes to marry her, she refuses. But now she already has the gift—which isn't fair. He asks for the gift back, and she refuses. This sends Apollo the God into a flying rage, because he feels betrayed by the lovely mortal, Cassandra. He wants to get his gift back, but he can't, because the gift was divine—meaning it was a divine power that he gave away, something that once given, can never be returned. He is suitably pissed off, and wants revenge on her, so he plans for bad things to happen to her, and for nobody to ever believe her again, so that even if she tries to prophesize, or tell any fortunes, her powers are rendered useless."

"Okaaay," Apollo said slowly, still not sure where Yiayia was going with this.

"My point, Apollo, is that what the God Apollo had to know and understand was that when he gave this gift away, he did so without expecting anything in return—because this, this is the true meaning of a gift. It's the same with love. When you choose to love, you have to know that this gift you are giving, you give away freely; you cannot put any expectations on it, any conditions, because when it is right, it just is. And when it's not right, it just isn't. We cannot control people, things. Love cannot be bought, or bargained for, the way Apollo the God tried to buy Cassandra's love. The good part out of all of this is that by not controlling things, then the things that are meant to be in your life will be there, because they are. This was the love I found with my Frank—your Papou—and this is the kind of love I want you to find for yourself, too. But mark my words: the right person who is meant to be in your life and share it with you will be there when the right time comes." She patted Apollo's leg then and got up off the bed and kissed him on the temple, wishing him a good sleep and saying she would see him in the morning.

The next morning, Apollo walked by to the back end of the school and broke down and cried like a baby for the best part of half an hour before gathering what little strength he had left to come back onto the school grounds. He was late, and when he walked into class, the teacher reprimanded him for it; the class knew he had been crying too, and some of the boys laughed and made derogatory comments, which made Apollo want to shrivel up and die on the spot. But the girls who who had once mocked him now took pity on him, and they felt for him seeing him so distraught like this. It had an affect on them, too, and they realised how much they had interfered with their nastiness, and how their cruelty had brought so much heartache. Apollo saw the girls whispering amongst one another when one of the girls, Natalie Vilden, a very pretty girl with strawberry blonde hair decided to make a play for Apollo. Class had finished and, at lunchtime, Apollo was walking across the footy field, alone and lost in his thoughts, when Natalie with her girlfriends walked over to him. Apollo, oblivious to their presence, was now sitting down thinking about his life, his future and what the point to it all was, when Natalie came up from behind the seats.

"She is not worth it, Apollo; you can do so much better, you little cutie," Natalie said, smiling. Apollo turned and looked at Natalie and the others standing with her.

"I don't want to 'do better' … I love her," Apollo replied honestly.

"Awww! Oh, poor boy," came the response from the group of girls standing there. They truly felt sad for him, and he could hear them murmuring how cute he looked, being all sad and depressed like that. Apollo just sat with his back to them, feeling vulnerable. Natalie came back and leaned over so that she was at his eye level.

"You could always use a new friend, Apollo—so why not talk to us? We can be your new friends, if you like?"

Apollo looked around the football field then looked back at the girls. "Sure, why not?" he replied half-heartedly, feeling disillusioned; with Alora gone he figured he had nothing else to lose.

Apollo got up and walked with them, following them back towards the school canteen. Natalie immediately grabbed his hand and they circled past the canteen to the eating area where all the students sat at an arrangement of tables. Apollo was too distracted and on too much of a downer to realise that Natalie and the girls, although attracted and interested in Apollo, were also wanting to show Alora that they now had him in their clutches. This, he suddenly realised, had been part of their plan from the get-go as Natalie led the gang past a series of tables, looking for Alora and holding onto Apollo's hand while parading around, flaunting their new friendship in Alora's face. Apollo locked eyes for a moment with Alora when he spotted her; in the awkwardness of the moment, they both quickly looked away. He knew he must have looked like a plaything for the girls too, and he could only guess what Alora must have been thinking. However, she said nothing; instead, she packed up her lunchbox and quietly left by the back door, which only made him feel even more like shit.

A week into their new friendship, Natalie invited Apollo over to her house; her parents were away for the weekend having gone to Kilcunda, a rural town near Inverloch, where they had a holiday caravan. Natalie's younger sister and older brother had also gone along on the trip, leaving the two home alone together at the family's home in Moonee Ponds.

"Hey, let's watch something fun," Natalie said, sorting through the family's movie collection. "I've got *The Princess Bride* and *Teen Wolf*, too—and you get to pick!"

"Okay," he shrugged, pointing to *The Princess Bride*.

"Haha! I thought for sure you were gonna pick *Teen Wolf*, being a guy," Natalie said, smirking. "I'll go get us some snacks—you start the movie," she said, bounding off to the kitchen. Moments later, she came back carrying a tray of junk food that included chips, chocolate, microwave pizza and coke. It all looked pretty disgusting to Apollo, but he took the coke and a handful of potato chips anyway, just to be polite.

They started watching *The Princess Bride*; when it got to the part where she was sitting on a log, defending her love for him, a quiet tear rolled down Apollo's face. True love, he thought, was hard to find; and even though he was sitting there next to this new girl, his heart was still Alora's.

Westley: Before his death I asked what was so important for him that he wanted to live, and he said, "True love."

"Do you want another soda?" Natalie asked innocently.

"Okay, sure," Apollo nodded.

"You're so cute and tiny," she said, stroking his face. "I'll be back in a minute," she said, getting up. Apollo cringed at the word 'tiny'. He could see that in his hurt, Natalie was merely a distraction, because he felt nothing for this girl, nothing at all. "You know," she said, pausing in the doorway, "Why don't we have a drink? My dad's got lots of alcohol! Let's have a couple of shots of Chartreuse. C'mon: it'll be fun!"

Apollo was reluctant to drink as he was a lightweight with alcohol, but wanting not to look like a wimp, he agreed.

"Oh, come on," Natalie said, nudging her foot across his stomach and playfully kicking and punching him. "One drink won't hurt."

Apollo consented. *Okay,* he reasoned with himself; then, *why not? One drink won't hurt, hey?* Natalie, all excited now, raced to her father's liquor cabinet and brought two drinks back to Apollo.

"Ready, set, down the hatch!" She said, giggling. They started with one shot and it hit him hard; unbeknownst to Apollo, Natalie had secretly poured him a double without pouring any for herself. Yet she feigned drinking to allure Apollo into believing that she was as well, so that he too skulled his shot, which made him cough and his head spin. Suddenly Apollo was feeling a little woozy, and then Natalie plied him with more; after the second shot he was very drowsy and no longer aware of his surroundings. Natalie got up and made her move on him then, kissing his neck, his throat, his face. Soon it was getting hot and heavy between them and, in his drunken state, Apollo accidentally called out Alora's name multiple times. Natalie slapped him hard, then aggressively pushed her foot across his throat as he lay there on the couch like a sack of potatoes.

"I am fucking Natalie, you little weasel! Stop calling her name—you're mine now." By now, Apollo couldn't remember where he was, and he soon passed out in front of her. Natalie lay there next to him, watching him as he slept; smiling devilishly, she climbed atop him and undid his pants. He was only half conscious through it all, and by the time she was finished, she climbed down off him feeling satisfied, having gotten what she wanted.

A few hours later, Apollo awoke, and when he realised what he had done, he broke down and cried out to the heavens above still in a drunken state.

"Oh, God—you're such a little sook! Get over it, will you? We are together now," she said, glowing at what they'd just done. She couldn't wait to tell everyone and for word to get around school—and especially for it to get back to Alora.

"What do you mean, 'we're together'? After just one week? I thought we were supposed to be friends?" Apollo mumbled, feeling puzzled. But he was a gentleman, and he didn't want to be perceived as the type to sleep with multiple girls; rather, he wanted to focus on one girl and cherish her and make it count. But Apollo knew he had to own his part in all this. It was he who, despite his hurt over Alora, had made the decision to come to Natalie's house and drink in the first place; and since he'd made that decision, it now seemed there was no turning back. He had succumbed to Natalie's wiles, and he had given her what she wanted—but now he needed to leave; he needed to go home and think about things. But, my God! The realisation also hit him just then that they'd had unprotected sex, and this truth sent him spinning; Apollo felt that he had betrayed Alora, even though she'd been the one who had betrayed and left him. Still, he couldn't shake the feeling that he had been unfaithful to her somehow, had cheated on her even, though deep down he knew in his heart he hadn't.

Apollo got on the phone to Yiayia, and trying to sound sober, asked if she could come pick him up, while Natalie told him that if he dared try to end it with her she would tell the school he willingly slept with her. She looked at him now with a cunning smile.

"I'd advise you to play along with this: the last thing you need is for Alora to catch wind of it," Natalie said, cornering him. *Hmmm, yes, the wind, the wind,* he thought to himself. Apollo's mind began to play Bob Dylan's *Blowin' in the Wind,* a song he'd caught Yiayia humming to many times.

Right then, Apollo knew he had just sealed his fate; there could be no chance of ever getting Alora back now, for this would all spread quickly. He'd ruined everything, and he knew it. The toot of Yiayia's horn interrupted his thoughts; Apollo raced out the front, hoping for a fast getaway, but Natalie closed the distance in on him, racing past him and reaching the car first.

"Hi there! How are you going, Mrs Pistakis, I am Natalie—it's so nice to meet you," she cooed, introducing herself. Angela shot Apollo a briefly confused look but smiled.

"Well, my grandson sure picks the pretty ones, doesn't he? I am Angela, and it's lovely to meet you, darling girl," Yiayia said politely. Natalie just smiled a cheeky, devious way and took Angela's hand in greeting.

"Thanks, you too—I am sure we will be seeing lots more of one another," she added, winking over at Apollo.

"Well bye now, Dear, glad you both had a fun movie night—I'm so happy my boy Apollo is getting out and about again!" Yiayia said cheerfully, starting the engine.

"Oh, me too, me too," Natalie said, stepping back from the car and waving them off.

***

After the weekend with Natalie, Apollo returned to school and suddenly found himself the target of many girls staring at him in the classroom. He could only imagine what Natalie had told them as they all sat there giggling mischievously with one another, occasionally taunting him. Natalie was seated up the front in the first row, smiling like the Cheshire Cat licking its paws as Alora entered the classroom, hand in hand with another student, an Italian boy. Guiseppe Gallichio was a tall, solid and well-built boy; Apollo had seen him around school sometimes, and, though he didn't know much about him, he thought he was an okay kid. But Apollo's heart fell out through his stomach; he couldn't believe what he was seeing. What the hell was Alora doing with him? Still, given what had just transpired between him and Natalie, he didn't really feel as though he had a right to know anyway, and feeling sheepish himself, Apollo lowered his head, pretending not to look. Still, he was surprised.

All through class, Apollo tried to stay focused, his attention divided between Natalie and Alora, but mostly on Alora; so he prayed for the bell to hurry up and ring and set him free from this hell. How had Alora found someone so quickly? Yet who was he to talk, having just slept with the first girl to come along himself, right after their break up? Of course, Apollo tried to justify this to himself, rationalising that he'd been thrown to the curb and had been left feeling hurt and vulnerable—but that excuse didn't really stick. The bell finally went, and Apollo realised he hadn't heard a word the teacher had said. One class down, one to go, he thought—he just had to get through PE and this nightmare of a day would be over.

Upon entering gym class, Apollo saw the basketball courts had already been set up with witches hats, ready to play poison ball for recreational activity. He walked to the drinking fountain for a quick drink then looked around, wanting to know where Alora was. Apollo liked this game because he was quick and nimble on his feet, which one needed to be in order to dodge the heavy, round medicine balls flying around. Within the first few minutes of the game, all the boys had all been struck out and it was just Apollo left with a handful of girls on the court. Gavin, Simon and Cale were up to their old tricks however, and they had taken this opportunity to get even with Apollo by filling the poison ball with added sand. Once the ball was heavy and overly weighted they started throwing it at Apollo, deliberately targeting him; but no matter how hard they tried, they just couldn't hit him with it—he was too fast, too agile and too good. Apollo was finally announced as the last man standing and won the game; once again he was getting the best of his tormentors, and it drove them wild with rage.

"Fucking midget! You short arse fucking wog!" Croosy bellowed at him across the court. Apollo walked off the court, even as he noticed Alora laughing along with them. Natalie too got stuck into him, gleefully enjoying the whole saga. Soon the entire class was tormenting Apollo, throwing slurs and derogatory names in his general direction. In that moment, Apollo was just about ready to fire up and fight back, when he remembered the wise words of the sensei floating back into his consciousness.

"Learn not to fight with anger, but with understanding."

The teacher, meanwhile, had gone off to grab his clipboard and missed the whole debacle, so the boys continued to let loose on Apollo even more.

"Why don't ya go back to your own country, fucking wog, 'coz we don't want yer here!" Croosy slurred, spitting at Apollo. But Apollo just stood there and took the abuse, because something much higher was coming to him now, and it was all of his learning with the sensei coming into practice, coming into real time.

Be strong on the inside and compassionate on the outside.

When these words entered Apollo's subconscious, he could suddenly see Croosy in a whole new light—and because of this, he knew there was no way he could fight this boy now, because the compassion he felt nullified every angry feeling he could have had towards the kid. Right now, all he could feel for Croosy was a deep sense of pity, sympathy even, for a kid so messed up that he hated himself and the world and everything in it. Apollo instead decided to walk over to him on his way out the door, and he did something so shocking that every kid in the room noticed.

"You're the best, Croosy. I really like you, man. You're just a freakin' legend."

But, seeing Alora laughing, that was what really broke his heart. That was what hurt the most. Not the word 'wog' or 'midget.' But as they kept chanting midget at him, Apollo walked out of that gym with his head held high and his dignity intact because he'd finally done something he could never do before—he reversed Croosy's bullying with compassion instead of violence, and he was using all of the sensei's teachings for good, instead of seeking revenge. And it felt good.

But there was still nothing worse than getting looked at,

getting seen. People making fun of him, making fun of his family, his Greekness.

But Yiayia knew Apollo's struggles now, and she would build him up every time he got bullied. Sometimes, in the past, Apollo had even felt like killing himself when he'd kept all the bullying to himself. But now that he had Yiayia, she'd say: "You're special. You are loved. Look right back at them. Talk your shit. Defend yourself. Then do it again. Understand your size abilities, not disabilities. Even a six or seven-footer isn't perfect; they have different height challenges, and what they can't do, you can. You can dribble low. You can steal that ball the moment it hits the ground. So, okay—you've got no choice but to dribble low. But you gotta make them come down to you. Make them play your ball game—and then see them struggle. Because you're already down there. This is your world. This is where you live. Make them meet you on your turf. My God, if your grandmother had been there today they woulda heard me talking my shit, 'coz I woulda been saying 'My grandson is smaller than all of you—and he's kicking your ASS!'"

"Yeah, but there's not much you can do with a hundred people cruelly chanting 'midget' at you—I hated even being out there on the court."

"That's why you gotta serve it right back to them, but do it honestly, do it with compassion, just like your sensei is teaching you—make them respect you. When they call you midget, agree and tell them all about your abilities. When they call you wog, agree with them and say, 'Yes, I am a wog.' Then proudly tell them all about your history, your roots, where you are from. Apollo mou! It's important to know your history! Why do you think Yiayia tells you all these things? You look Greek, you sound Greek, you speak Greek, you are Greek—look, you even squeeze lemon over everything you eat, just the way your great-grandfather used to! We cannot deny our heritage—and we should never deny our history or be ashamed of it, because we all have one. It is a fundamental part of who you are; it is the sum of you. This is not to say you are not Aussie too, because you live here now and this is your home—but that doesn't make you any less Greek," she said, adjusting her hair bun. Apollo nodded. As with every word she ever spoke, Yiayia always spoke the truth.

She was truly the moral muscle of the family, and Apollo didn't know what he'd do without her.

CHAPTER FIFTEEN

A Pregnant Pause

Every second year the school had a variety night they celebrated in December, where the students could all come dressed up as whomever or whatever they wanted to be. Natalie called Apollo and told him that she was late, but Apollo didn't catch on right away or understand what that meant, and so assumed that she had meant she would be arriving late to the variety night.

"No, you stupid goof! I am late because I missed my period! You got me pregnant, you dumbass!" Apollo was speechless; in fact, he was in such a state of shock that he couldn't bring himself to say a word. There was nothing but dead silence on the other end of the line.

"Cat got your tongue, eh, Greek boy?" Natalie mocked. "Well, I am pregnant with your baby; just thought you should know, hey." Apollo had to admit, pregnant or not, this girl was a funky punky brewster even at the best of times, and she had a mouth and a 'tude so edgy she could make grown men cry.

"I will be coming with you to the variety night, so make sure you get your Yiayia to pick me up, because we have to go together." Apollo was devastated; while Natalie prattled on mindlessly as though nothing was the matter, Apollo felt his whole world collapsing all around him, right before his very eyes. He felt like Edmund Dantès in his favourite book, *The Count of Monte Cristo*, locked away in a prison, a dungeon for so many years, buried under the rubble, crushed by the weight of his own sins and others', with no possible way out. He remembered how close Edmund had come to giving up too, but how with a stone he'd carved the words 'God Will Give Me Justice' into the wall each and every day because he knew that holding onto this one belief was what would keep him alive. Apollo didn't feel the need to seek revenge or justice on what Natalie or anyone for that matter had done to him now, because now he finally understood that God was going to take care of things for him anyway, in His own good time and that God would never leave him.

He put the phone down and called out to Yiayia; in fact, he didn't call, he screamed. Yiayia came running, because the scream was just so bloodcurdling she thought Apollo must have hurt himself. Upon seeing her grandson standing there in his bedroom unharmed, she said, "I'll be back in just a minute—I've got cooking on the stove, and, if I don't take it off right now, the heat will ruin everything!" Yiayia shot off down the hall and Apollo just sat there; his head felt as though he were in a goldfish bowl, with little goldfish swimming erratically in all different directions.

When Yiayia returned to his bedroom, Apollo broke down and told her everything that had been happening at school; then he told her that Natalie was pregnant and the baby was his. Yiayia looked stunned, but she took him in her arms and hugged him for the longest time.

"You know, Apollo, life is never easy—but you're a survivor, and no matter what life throws at you, you can always bounce back, no matter what. For as long as you still have life inside of you, there is always hope, my darling," she explained calmly.

Apollo smiled and nodded; Yiayia always managed to make him feel as though no mountain was ever too big to climb, because in her mind everything was always possible.

"I'm scared though, Yiayia," Apollo whispered, feeling uncertain about everything.

"It's okay, Apollo—we are family, and we will always support each other and be there for each other, in good times and bad. Nothing is ever insurmountable—and this won't be the first—or the last—challenge life ever throws at you. But let's talk more about it later, because right now you have to go get ready to go to the variety event—and now we need to pick up Natalie on the way, too," she said, being suddenly all businesslike.

Apollo showered and they picked up Natalie on the way; she was hormonal and in a bad mood, but Apollo reassured her that he would support her and that she wasn't alone.

"That's right," Yiayia seconded, calming Natalie down. "My grandson isn't a quitter, nor is he a pig that would shy away from any decisions or run from his responsibilities," she said with finality. "Natalie, Apollo and I will support you through this, and we will be there for you, but we are all going to need lots of help too, because clearly Apollo isn't ready for this either. So let's all be kind to each other through this journey, and we will all get through it together, in one piece," she said, driving in through the school's gates.

"I do want to keep the baby," Natalie said quietly, sitting in the back seat next to Apollo.

"And have you told your parents about this yet?" Yiayia wanted to know.

"Yes—my parents support my decision, but they want to meet Apollo, because they want to know who it was that got their daughter pregnant. But they weren't angry about it—they were pretty laid back about it actually, which surprised me because I thought my dad might kick me out. But he just said that it was common that most kids my age were exploring their sexuality, and he said he would support my decision, whatever I decided to do."

"Well, it sounds as though your father has a good head on his shoulders," Yiayia said, stopping the car. "Listen: for the moment I want you two to promise me you'll go and have fun at this thing tonight and put this out of your minds, and we will talk more about it tomorrow—because right now I need to rush home to Papou; he hasn't been well and he still can't shake this blasted cold," she said, quickly driving away. Apollo and Natalie agreed that they would do as she'd asked, and they made off in the direction of the school's main hall where, even from a distance, they could already hear the night's event in full swing.

Apollo entered, looking up at the lights and music playing in the background, and immediately spotted Alora, who was over by the far wall, standing with Guiseppe.

They made their way to the drinks bar, Apollo poured two drinks and handed one to Natalie. As soon as he took the first sip, he knew it had been spiked. *Croosy, I'll bet*, he thought to himself. "Natalie, you can't drink this," he said, taking the drink out of her hand. Now with two drinks for himself, they went and sat down at a nearby table. He closed his eyes and wished he were back in Cyprus living a different life to the one that he now had; how he wished this were all just a nightmare that he could make disappear.

Instead, he opened his eyes and was disappointed to find he was still at the variety night, and now Natalie was slapping him on the head.

"Hey, what the fuck is wrong with you?" she whined, playing with her long strawberry locks. "Why do you keep closing your eyes like that? Are you tired? C'mon and stay awake tonight, hey; don't fall asleep on me like you did when we were together last."

Apollo sighed; there was no point arguing with her, so he pretended he was going to the bathroom, and instead went to the drinks bar to have more punch when she wasn't looking. They sat through some of the performances that had been organised for the night; one was a clown who performed illusions using fireballs and sticks, wowing and dazzling the crowd with his juggling skills; another was an older girl who sang opera, and yet another act were twin ventriloquists with their dummies. At the interval everyone moved towards the refreshment table and light buffet; Apollo excused himself again to Natalie, explaining that he just wanted some time alone, and he wandered over to the other end of the hall, where it was quieter, skulling yet another glass of punch. He came upon a small door leading backstage, and in his inebriated state he went through and sat down and cried out to God, asking why he'd made such a mess of his life, why he'd had to go and ruin it all. Unbeknownst to him, Alora had followed Apollo over and was now right behind him, worried about his current state. Apollo looked up, surprised to see her.

"Get lost," he told her, lashing out at her against his better judgment. Deep down he was ecstatic to see her, but his pride would have nothing of it. "What do you fucking want, and why aren't you with your boyfriend?" he slurred.

"I'm sorry," Alora told him, "I'm just worried about you: you're drunk, and I've been watching you slamming drinks all night … it's not like you," she said tenderly, offering him her hand. But Apollo pulled away.

"Where's your new boyfriend—why aren't you with him?" Apollo barked back.

"Because: I just told you—I was worried about you."

"Okay, well let me ask you this, dear sweet Alora: have you remained faithful to your promise to your mother, or have broken that too, with the new boyfriend?" he asked sarcastically. Alora was so hurt by Apollo's accusation she grabbed him by the throat and threatened to punch him, even though he knew she would never do such a thing. Instead, she served the same accusation back on him.

"Yeah, well I know what happened—actually the entire school knows—what happened with you and Natalie; but I know you were drunk, and she admitted to me that she'd played you, so I don't hold it against you," she said, releasing her grip.

"She said she'd played me?"

"Apollo, I am so sorry, but I still love you, I do—my problem is I worry too much about what other people think," Alora confessed, her voice filled with sadness and regret. Hearing her voice now, and knowing her as well as he did, reached Apollo's heart; he immediately softened, realising only she could have this affect on him.

"I understand, peer pressure is hard—I can understand that," he said, finally accepting her hand.

"I still love you, Apollo, and my feelings haven't changed," she said softly, and before they knew it, they were kissing. Alora was drunk as well and Apollo knew all too well that the truth always came out when people were drunk and vulnerable. He felt disoriented in his life and in the world, and he didn't know where to turn; only Alora could be his rock; she was the one thing that anchored him, the one thing he felt he could hold onto when he felt himself drifting out to sea. He held onto her now.

"Oh Alora, my Alora, I am so sorry," he moaned miserably, wanting to kiss her again. "What have I done? I've ruined everything. Yes, I slept with Natalie, and I had no right to attack you about Guiseppe—but I have to tell you something: Natalie is pregnant."

"Oh my God—you're kidding me, right?" Alora sat back in shock; she had to take all this in. "How—how do you feel about all this?"

"Alora—please, it was an accident; I don't love Natalie, but now I will have to do the right thing and stand by her …"

"She's such a slut! She sleeps with every boy in school! She's totally played you!" Alora said again, heartbroken. She shook her head at the tragedy of the whole situation.

"I'd like to give you a birthday kiss if I may; it's your seventeenth birthday next week, you know," he said, and Alora was so touched by the fact that he hadn't forgotten that she leapt into his arms. Meanwhile, out in the main hall, Natalie was searching everywhere for Apollo, and Guiseppe was now wondering the same about Alora.

Unbeknownst to the both of them, the clown that had before been playing with the magic fireballs was now drunk from the punch as well and, not knowing that one of the fireballs was still lit and near one of the stage curtains, he stumbled to his feet, leaving them behind, as Apollo and Alora continued kissing, the little ball of fire flickering just metres away. If Alora and Apollo hadn't been so engulfed in their own passions they would have noticed the kindling flame in the corner about to engulf them; instead, they made out until they passed out in each other's arms. But the room was now heating up and the flames had manifested as a large fire was scaling around them, surrounding them both as the curtains danced symbolically around them like fiery, burning men brandishing dangerous swords.

There were screams of panic as the fire brigade arrived with everyone evacuating the hall and moving to the nearest exit points. Meanwhile, a search party had been sent out to look for Apollo and Alora, who were eventually discovered half-naked and sweating on the floor backstage in each other's arms, drunk and shrouded in smoke. The paramedics raced them both to the hospital to treat them for smoke inhalation and minor injuries, and Yiayia flew into a panic and became hysterical herself, racing to the hospital upon receiving the news that her grandson had been admitted.

***

Troy and Angela sat by Apollo's bedside, holding his hand while he slept, attached to an oxygen mask. Yiayia watched the delicate rise and fall of the bag inside the ICU ventilator as it marked time with Apollo's every breath, and it reminded her of the inexplicable beauty and cosmic simplicity of the act of breathing, and its sweet representations of life itself. Alora was in the next room along down the hall with similar injuries, surrounded by her family.

"We had to perform some light manual resuscitation of the patient with an ambu bag, but he will be fine now—they are both extremely lucky, because it could have been a hell of a lot worse," the doctor explained to Yiayia, upon entering the room. "That said, we'd like to keep them both in overnight for observation, just to be on the safe side." Yiayia was nodding in agreement when Natalie burst into the room, fuming.

"Why was he alone with that bitch?" she spat, but but no-one knew what was going on, and Natalie, now in a full-blown rage, began cursing, saying how she was going to make Apollo pay for what he'd done to her.

"I don't know what you're talking about, young lady—but I'd like to remind you that this here is my grandson you are talking about, all while he lies here in a serious, if not critical condition," Yiayia glared at the girl, admonishing her for her tactlessness.

"There, there, Yiayia is here," she said, stroking Apollo's singed arm.

"Where am I?" Apollo asked drowsily.

"Everything's okay, darling—you are just in the hospital for observation, and Troy and I are right here with you, just rest."

"But Alora—where is she?" Apollo struggled to speak, mumbling out from under the mask.

Angela calmed him down, replying, "Yes darling, Alora is okay; she is in the next room to you, it's all going to be okay." But hearing Yiayia speak about Alora only enraged Natalie more.

"Why are you asking about her? I am the one who is pregnant with your baby! You're mine, you little Greek shit!" Angela turned to face Natalie, her face a mixture of horror and disbelief.

"We need to stay calm right now, Natalie—you seem to be forgetting that you are in a hospital ... Please show some respect."

Apollo was becoming more conscious due to the screaming. He tried to sit up. "Where is Alora? Where is Papou?" he asked again, worried. Just then, Mary and Mateus arrived. Apollo took one look at his mother and started screaming hysterically.

"What is she doing here? Get out! Get out! I don't want to see her! Fucking hypocrite!" He yelled maniacally at his mother.

"Apollo—wait," a dishevelled-looking Mateus countered, "Your mother came here because she cares about you, and I care about you, too … we were both so worried to hear that you were in hospital, and—"

"You can get out too—both of you! You ruined my life! You ruined my GODDAMN FUCKING LIFE!" Apollo screamed and blasted like a madman on crack. Everyone in the room looked suddenly shell-shocked; they had never seen Apollo so crazed, or so out of his wits. They all looked at Apollo then, his face red, his fists clenched by the bed. But Apollo was on a roll now, and there was no stopping him. He just kept flipping.

"You couldn't be bothered coming to my track meet—you weren't there for me through my hospitalisation, you weren't there for any fucking moments that mattered to me these last four years! Karate, the bullying I endured at school—you couldn't even remember to come to my fucking birthday! You gave birth to be, remember? And now you show up here, pretending to look all concerned and motherly? Fuck you! Fuck you! Get out! Get out!"

Mary made a slight step forward, wanting to hug her son, wanting to make up for everything, but Apollo looked ready to launch at her; instead, Mateus held up his hand to signal a ceasefire, then he grabbed Mary's arm, pulling her back towards the door.

"It's okay, Apollo, we're leaving, we didn't mean to upset you—we apologise, son. Be well," he said, still holding Mary by the arm and dragging her out.

Apollo lay back in the hospital bed, shaking and spent from his sudden outburst and instantly regretting what he'd done. He didn't know what had overcome him. Well, so much for all of the sensei's teachings on being able to control his mind, he thought. He looked over at Yiayia, and seeing the darkness now stricken across her face, quickly apologised, but Yiayia herself could only hang her head low in shame. To see her family so divided, so broken like this went against everything she believed in, undid all the work she'd done in wanting to bring her family together again in the same country. It was her worst nightmare come true.

"Thank God your Papou was not here to see this," was all she could muster.

"It's okay, bro, don't feel bad—c'mon, you know we have two spastic losers for parents, don't let them upset you, don't let them get to you," Troy said, trying to help.

"Troy—that will be enough!" Yiayia barked, even though she didn't disagree.

As the shame overwhelmed him, Apollo respectfully asked Yiayia if he could have some time alone, then called out to Natalie as the rest left the room. Natalie, being very intuitive, sensed Apollo was quick to forgive and could be easily controlled, and she took full advantage of it in the moment. She walked up to his bedside and grabbed him by the back of his hair.

"You are never to go near Alora again—or I will never let you near this baby once it's born," she seethed. Apollo, still fuming at his own mother, painfully agreed and promised Natalie that he wouldn't. He would never abandon this baby the way he'd been abandoned. He just wouldn't.

CHAPTER SIXTEEN

The Dawn of a New Era

On the eve of 1990, at the turn of a new year, Apollo sat under the stars by the old lemon tree in Angela and Frank's garden, reminiscing on previous New Year's Eves he'd spent with Alora in simpler times. But that was in the past now, for this year would be the dawn of a new era as Apollo faced new responsibilities with impending fatherhood and a baby on the way. School had started back and he and Natalie were now settling into a new future together; Natalie had by now moved in to Frank and Angela's house and was going to school part-time on a special teenage mother's pregnancy program so that she could continue her learning while having the baby, and Apollo was just trying to get through his final year of high school.

Apollo would often see Alora at school, though usually it was from a distance and she was always with Guisseppe; painfully he had to admit to himself that he'd lost her, even though he still had a hard time accepting it. Then suddenly, one day in February 1990, Alora's father abruptly came into the school, and without warning, removed Alora from the school completely. No-one knew what was going on or the reasons behind it, but Apollo grieved, shattered by the thought that he might never see her again, even from a distance. Then, he gathered his composure and willed himself to commit to Natalie—one who wasn't his first choice, but was carrying his child. No, he was determined to be a good, if not great, father to this child, despite being young himself. He had a ways to go, but Apollo was slowly maturing, and the knowledge that he was about to become a father loomed as not only a huge responsibility, but a reality check.

He sat with Papou one Saturday afternoon while Natalie had gone shopping for baby clothes; it would be man to man talk, with Papou dishing out his usual wisdom and humour that Apollo so loved him for. Papou was still very sick, and Apollo served his grandfather hot tea as he sat in his favourite recliner wrapped in his favourite Carlton football club scarf.

"I'm eighty-seven now, but the old ticker's still working, still going strong," Papou joked, sending himself into an unexpected coughing fit. He asked Apollo for his pills, and Apollo had to gently remind Papou that he'd given them to him just an hour ago. Yiayia was convinced Papou also had the beginnings of dementia going on, but joked that half the time she thought she did too, forever forgetting where she was putting things.

"Never let your left hand know what your right hand is doing, son," Papou declared, and Apollo smiled to himself, having heard this a thousand times before; it was one of his most favourite and wisest sayings.

"When I was your age, I put my head down and worked hard because my goal was to get into real estate; those were busy times, to be sure, because your Yiayia was pregnant and we were just trying to scrape by. But we made it, and I know you will do the same—just put your head down and work hard, and don't forget to enjoy yourself along the way," he smiled in between coughs. "Ah, the days when I whisked your grandmother off to the vineyards, going for long drives through the countryside. Those were the best days …"

Papou took a long sip of tea then leaned back and rested his head against the headrest. Apollo took in his grandfather's face as if noticing him for the first time; he saw the aging then, followed the deep traces of lines that now marked his cheeks, his temple. How had he not seen his grandfather's aging before? To him he had just always been the jovial, lively Papou he'd always known. He'd been as close a surrogate father as one could get, and he meant the world to Apollo. Papou thought for a moment, then continued: "There are four things you must never loan out to anybody in this lifetime—your wife, your car, your house or your money."

"Oh, Papou, that's a good one, that's funny," Apollo said, smiling. "Okay, I won't—promise."

"You know, son, I don't think I ever really learned that much in this life; I wasn't as smart or as educated as you young boys are today—but I did work hard, and your grandmother and I made a nice life for ourselves out here. The one thing I do know—I think it was Napoleon who first said it, and this is something I think about often—is the fact that we are all either kings or pawns in this life. You always have the power to choose: you can be the lead role in your own life or an extra in someone else's. Be a king," he winked. "As for the rest of it, it's all Greek to me," he said, shrugging his shoulders and laughing at his own joke.

"Feel like a game of backgammon then, King?" Apollo nudged his grandfather tenderly.

"Not right now, son; I think I just need a rest," Papou mumbled, closing his eyes, aware that his time on earth was growing shorter with each passing day.

By July, Natalie's waters broke and she was off to the hospital in a hurry; after forty-seven hours of excruciating labour, she gave birth to a little boy, Jordan. Natalie cried for joy and Apollo took the little baby boy in his arms, gobsmacked by how beautiful he was. Apollo couldn't believe this child was his, and it suddenly hit him, the stark realisation that he was now a father. They had decided on the name Jordan because Natalie had always loved it, and Apollo thought he was just perfect as he sat and delicately cradled ten small fingers and ten little toes in the palms of his hands. He was completely smitten with the bundle of joy he now held in his arms; with tears in his eyes he gazed upon his newborn son, then back to Natalie.

"We did it, babe. We did it. Wow. You were so amazing! I am just speechless with gratitude; I am so proud of you. Thank you for all you have done, thank you for this incredible gift you have given us," Apollo said humbly, leaning over the bed to plant a kiss on Natalie's forehead. She looked as any new mother would after having endured endless hours of labour; her hair was a mess, her eyes withdrawn, her skin pale, her body limp. But Natalie managed a weak smile for Apollo, acknowledging him in the moment, relieved it was finally over with.

"She really does need a lot of rest at the moment," the rotund nurse stated firmly, taking in all the people that had descended upon Room 213. Troy, Angela, Frank and Mary were all there and eager to meet the newest addition to the family; even Mateus,

Olivia and Alan had arrived to congratulate Apollo and Natalie for the beautiful miracle of life they had created and brought into the world. Apollo knew that no amount of explaining to the nurse could ever make her understand that this was just the way it was in Greek families; they always gathered in droves, because this was just how things were done, it was the Greek way—and they especially liked to come together whenever it had anything to do with births, weddings and funerals—because simply put, Greeks were not known to do anything by halves. Apollo nodded anyway, understanding and acknowledging the nurse's orders, assuring her he would have the room cleared out shortly so that Natalie could rest.

Frank and Angela took turns at holding baby Jordan. "Well, I have to be honest with you," Yiayia began, "he looks a lot like Natalie, though I suppose it's too early yet to see any resemblance to you, Apollo—but he definitely has Natalie's eyes, that's for sure," she said, nodding and looking down into baby Jordan's wonderfully innocent, big eyes that were now staring right back at her.

"Yes, and I do see a tinge of Natalie's reddish gold flecks in his hairline, too, don't you think?" Mary noted, cooing over the newborn. However, Apollo didn't care one bit what his mother thought; this was his son now and he couldn't wait to teach him all the things his father never had, make up for all the things he felt he had missed out on. Apollo immediately felt his mind jumping forward like a movie reel, and he could already picture himself in a park with Jordan, teaching his son how to catch a ball on a sunny day, or digging in the sand together making sandcastles up to the sky. Apollo was already so dedicated and devoted to this new baby that he would make becoming a father his life's work.

Things between Apollo and his mother had been tense since the hospital, and Apollo had scarcely said a word to her. He felt guilty for the way he'd acted too, even though to him it had been fully justified. *God will give you justice,* Apollo had reckoned the following day, though he realised he had been wrong in seeking it himself, failing to apply all the lessons he had learned through Sensei. Apollo nodded to himself; now he had the chance to right things, and this was the right moment. He channelled the wisdom of the sensei now, willing it to overtake him, willing it to drive out his desire for revenge, the way Edmund Dantès had been so fixated on doing in *Monte Cristo.* Now he was determined that, if he should see Croosy at school, he would fight him only with love; and if he saw Alan or Mary, he would show compassion and come only from a place of understanding. He knew that this was a tall order, but all the hate that had built up inside of him over the years was now only hurting him—and he determined himself to be rid of it, because he finally understood that all of the power he had sought to find had been right there all along: within.

In the coming days, Apollo and Natalie left the hospital with a newborn baby and a new addition to their young family in their arms. As was Greek tradition, the family gathered at home again to welcome the new baby properly, and Yiayia cooked up a magnificent Greek feast, this time including some local Australian fare such as sausage rolls and meat pies to cater for their Australian friends who had also been invited to join in the celebrations.

Apollo pulled his mother aside, asking her to join him in the garden. He felt he had so much to say to her; there was still so much water to let under the bridge, and in the spirit of a new era, he just needed to clear the air once and for all.

"I am sorry for my outburst in the hospital that day, and I realise now that you were genuinely concerned for me," Apollo began, in an attempt to break the ice between them.

"Oh, Apollo—I am the one who is sorry for failing you both as a mother these past few years; it took me a long time to realise why too, and to snap out of whatever I was going through. It's painful for me to admit to this, even now—but I think I transferred my hatred of Mateus onto you boys because you—especially you, Apollo—were the spitting image of your father. And I was angry, I was so angry at him too, for the way he treated me back then, when we first came to Australia—"

"It's okay, really. I understand," Apollo said, cutting Mary off and forgiving her, because what he'd wanted so badly right then was for her to know that he really, truly, finally had.

Mateus came out to join them then. He had overheard part of their conversation, and in the same spirit of forgiveness he put his arm around Mary and Apollo. "Let me please say that I too am sorry for the part I own in this whole mess, for mistreating you, Mary, and for abandoning you boys. It wasn't right what we did, and I can only vow to be a better parent now, moving forward. Mary, can you believe our son is now a father? This makes us grandparents! Maybe that's why I feel so old … " he said, jokingly grabbing at his back. "I think a toast to our Apollo is in order—congratulations, son! Opa!" he declared, raising his glass to the sounds of cheers and clinking. "Ee-gia mas!" they all said, cheering.

Before Apollo left, he told his parents it was all okay; he wasn't angry anymore, and he understood that his parents had had their own story and their own struggles that had caused them to make the awful decisions they had made in abandoning their sons. *Come from a place of compassion and understanding, not judgment, and you will see more, understand more,* the words of the sensei came to him over and over again. Apollo realised he was just super grateful to have his entire family, parents and grandparents on board with him now; it just made life so much easier. He secretly thanked Sensei too, for showing him the way out beyond the darkness and into the light. Just as the celebrations came to a close, and just as everyone was preparing to leave, Apollo finally built up the courage to approach his tormentor Alan, offering up an outstretched hand.

"I just want to thank you for coming today, Alan," Apollo said, channelling Sensei's words about compassion, "and I wanted to apologise to you for being a bit of a brat and a bit difficult when I was younger—but really, I was just a typical kid struggling so much with my parent's separation at the time, you know? And I also want you to know that I forgive you too, for tormenting me and attacking me and putting a bag on my head—just stuff like that, you know—because you were also thrown into parenting, and you had no idea how to be a parent back then, either. I just hope you can continue being a great father to Maggie now," Apollo said sincerely, looking Alan directly in the eye and speaking as one father to another.

Apollo's maturity in the moment clearly caught Alan off guard and blew him away because Alan began to sweat, and his eyes jumped around the room playing its own game of aversion as he tried to mumble something even vaguely as mature in reply; but Apollo could see Alan's uneasiness, looking like he couldn't wait to get out the door, and this was enough payback for Apollo, for in seeing Alan squirm like that, he knew he had finally settled the score between them. Yet who could have known how much power and healing could come in originating from a place of kindness, a kindness so foreign to Alan it had made his skin crawl? *God will give you justice,* a faraway voice seemed to whisper again to Apollo.

***

The next couple of months were hard as Apollo and Natalie were met with the new challenges of parenting and starting a new life together, but Apollo was relishing fatherhood as he continued with his studies and found himself a job on Saturday mornings as a casual factory hand. It was repetitive work assembling circuit boards, but it paid well. He continued with his martial arts when money would allow, and as the months wore on Apollo had saved enough to be able to move out with Natalie and Jordan and build a family of their own. They found a little apartment not far from his grandparents, and Apollo left school to take up an apprenticeship as a repair technician where he repaired telecommunications equipment, fax machines, photocopiers and cordless phones. Again, it paid very well and he was able to support Natalie and baby Jordan, although by now he had stopped training in martial arts and was focusing all his energies on them, wanting to be the best father and partner he could be.

Natalie often left Apollo at home with baby Jordan in the evenings after spending all day with baby as a stay-at-home mum, but Apollo didn't mind; in fact, he loved that he got to spend quality time bonding with his son after work hours. Many a night Apollo would spend hours just cuddling and playing with Jordan; he loved feeding him and assisting with changing nappies and rocking him to sleep, and more often than not Natalie would return home after a night out with friends to baby Jordan snoring happily in his tired father's arms, as he and Apollo nodded off together in front of the TV. But Apollo took it all in stride, and he felt it was a pleasure and delight to be a man and do whatever he could for Natalie by easing the load around the house, even doing all the shopping and paying bills. By Christmas, Apollo had turned into quite the domesticated house-partner, working full shifts by day and running a tight ship at home by night.

"I don't see you much anymore, man, what's happened to you?" Troy complained to Apollo one day. "Yiayia is complaining too, that she hasn't hardly seen boo of you lately, either! She told me to tell you that she is going to come by this weekend and bring you moussaka for Sunday dinner, okay, bro?"

Apollo nodded; he was grateful for the strong support of his family but he wanted to prove to himself and that he could do this with little to no help from them. As the months wore on, Apollo strived to build what he thought was the perfect family home life; he had saved hard for a deposit for a house and had already hired a bunch of tradespeople to work on it. He was involved in every stage of its construction as it was being built too, and everything was going perfectly to schedule as they looked set to finish the property in the projected six-month time frame. There had even been a little money left over, which meant that Apollo could buy Natalie the new car she had been wanting. Apollo kept working smarter and harder all the time, juggling his responsibilities by day as a breadwinner and provider with his role as a father by night. Baby Jordan had all the stories and toys he could desire and was by all accounts a seemingly intelligent baby boy, hitting all his developmental milestones, which pleased Apollo to no end. No kid of his would ever be developmentally slow, and he made sure to meet his every need, because nothing was ever too much or too difficult in his eyes. By six months of age Jordan had started to utter his first words, "Mama and Baba," which meant mother and father in Greek. He taught Jordan Greek words whenever Natalie was off at the gym and Yiayia sang songs to her great-grandson whenever they visited. Life was finally good and enjoyable and Apollo felt that Australia had served him well in the end, rising above all the hardships he had faced in the early years.

"I swear, Apollo, I have yet to see a more dedicated or devoted father than you," Yiayia proudly announced one day. "This baby is blessed to have you for a father, I tell you! But you must promise me to take care of yourself too, for you are no good to this family if you go getting yourself sick from pushing yourself and working so hard."

"It's okay, Yiayia—really it is. I'm happy and healthy and we are all doing just fine," Apollo said, trying to reassure her. Natalie did not like Yiayia's constant meddling ways, but Apollo knew his grandmother only ever cared about them and he never once saw her as overbearing or meddling. Only kind. Perhaps Natalie just struggled with the closeness of his tight-knit Greek family because her family had never been that close so she had never really known what a tight-knit family unit looked like. Still, the parenting trail was full of learning and surprises and it had all been worth it after all, because Apollo had learned some valuable life experiences along the way, though nothing could ever be better than this miracle of life both he and Natalie had created. Natalie bounded into the kitchen just then all sweaty from her workout, and upon seeing Jordan resting in Yiayia's lap she scooped him up into her arms.

"There's my big boy!" she cried, adorning Jordan's rosy cheeks with kisses. Apollo could see how childbirth had changed Natalie for the better; she had become more empathetic, softer around the eyes somehow, mellowing into motherhood. He had started to develop real feelings for Natalie too, as his compassion for her grew; beyond her harsh exterior there lay a vulnerable and insecure woman Apollo could now see through the gift of Sensei's eyes. People, Apollo realised, were often not what they seemed, and he paused then, remembering Croosy. Back in high school days Croosy had seemed larger than life, an ogre, a monster—whereas now all Apollo could see was a frightened, insecure kid with no home life who had just wanted to be popular, wanted to be loved. He knew that Croosy had always been ignored at home, cast aside as though he were nothing more than a nuisance, in the way—and in a way, he had bullied Apollo as a way of getting the attention he'd been so starved of on the home front—because, even to Croosy, negative attention was better than being invisible or getting no attention at all. As a parent, Apollo now fully understood this, which was why he gave all his attention to baby Jordan and Natalie, because no-one ever deserved to feel unloved like that; not even Croosy.

Apollo was proud of how far he had come in just a few short years; after all, he now had a beautiful son and the mother of his child who he was becoming quite fond of, making a real little family and having a roof over their heads, a place to call home. Frank and Angela frequently visited and even Mary and Alan would call by or stop in for afternoon tea and cake, despite the differences they'd shared in the past. Troy was a loving uncle to his little nephew and Apollo enjoyed spending simple times with his family; these moments, he realised, were what he lived for, and they were the most beautiful moments of all. Maybe now Apollo could finally dare to dream for greater things to come his way; maybe now the stars had finally aligned in his favour.

"We are the kings of Limassol!" Troy declared walking in the door, having just wrapped up a session of weights, looking like a Greek God.

"Yeah, bro, yeah we are the kings—be a king, not a pawn!" Apollo smiled.

CHAPTER SEVENTEEN

Beauty and the Beast

"Baba! Mama!" little Jordan squealed with delight as he half-toddled, half-stumbled towards his parents across the playground. The Australian sun was shining brightly overhead as Apollo opened his arms wide, embracing his son and scooping up this little boy so full of energy and life. Jordan was a happy and beautiful little boy now, with many people stopping to comment on his great and striking features. It made Apollo feel proud, and it brought him back to his own fleeting childhood memories of being a young boy playing out on the cobbled streets of Cyprus with his young friend, Massimo, in what felt like a lifetime ago. What he would give to see Massimo now, he thought.

But time passes just as it always does, and Apollo had watched on intently as Jordan began to grow; slowly he had risen to his feet as he'd learned to balance; then he had learned how to get on tippy toes to reach whatever he had wanted from the kitchen bench. Soon enough he had learned to toddle, and then to walk—and before long, and before Apollo knew it, in the blink of an eye, Jordan was running and chasing birds through the park or down a hill after a runaway ball. Life was like that, Apollo thought. You've just got to learn to crawl before you can walk, and sometimes it takes tripping and falling over a few times in life before you eventually get the hang of it. And Jordan was as active a little boy as Apollo had ever been, which convinced him that he must have got his running legs and agility from him. He couldn't explain all the intricate nuances of fatherhood or how it made him feel, for there were just too many to count; it just made him so proud.

"I really think we need to discuss the possibility of putting Jordan down for soccer classes," Apollo suggested lightly to Natalie one day.

"Oh, I don't know, Apollo—why not football or cricket, that's much more popular here than soccer … you're not in Europe, you know," came Natalie's wry reply. But Apollo didn't really care if it was soccer or football or music lessons or anything else; he just had so many dreams for his son and it felt like they were only just scratching the surface with all the ideas, possibilities and desires of the heart when it came to wishing things for his son's bright future.

"I'm going out again tonight with the girls, so if you could please clean up the dirty plates in the kitchen when you get back that would be great," Natalie said sweetly, giving Apollo a quick peck on the cheek as she was leaving. Apollo nodded, he would often do all the house chores because he wanted to ensure that Natalie never went without or felt undesired; after all, it was his job to make sure she and Jordan were loved and cared for, keeping his little family happy and safe.

But by 1993, Apollo and Natalie were beginning to have some very real problems, because she wanted to have more kids and Apollo wanted to wait, at least until they were more financially settled. He had come to love Natalie despite her many flaws and controlling habits, and he just wanted to take things slow and give all his energy and time to the young family he already had; besides, things were busy enough as they were, what with one child, and life was expensive enough, even with just one. Apollo had developed into that of a striking young man of significantly larger stature and strong, handsome Cypriot features, by now regularly hitting the local gym three times a week with his brother Troy, and it was nice that he could finally carve out just a little free time for himself. Both boys were by now chiselled men, having really come into their own skin, and Apollo's strength and confidence had grown exponentially with every bench press he'd lifted. But life always has a habit of throwing curveballs, even when things are seemingly good and great, and the next day was no exception.

It was a crisp day late in August just as winter's long-bellied grey days rounded themselves into springtime's blush, and the air smelled fragrant and light with the bloom of cherry blossoms and tulips dancing in the wind to the change of seasons. Apollo was sitting in the living room reading the paper as was his usual Saturday morning routine when he thought he saw his dream job in the community services section; listed was a traineeship in aged care and nursing with a caption at the bottom: "No Experience Required." He thought about the pact he'd made with Alora a lifetime ago to chase their dreams, and while it wasn't exactly in the medical field, it was close enough, so he decided to apply for it. The money looked impressive too, plus it offered on-the-job-training, and the career opportunities seemed endless.

A few days later, Apollo had been contacted for an interview; so, on September 18th, 1993, Apollo showered, shaved, dressed and headed off in the direction of the airport, where the head office was located. As he drove himself to the interview, Taylor Dayne's song, *Love Will Lead You Back* started to play on the car's radio, and even Apollo had to admit that it was pretty ironic that this place was not far from where his entire journey to Australia had begun way back in 1986, nearly eight years ago. When Apollo arrived he was escorted to a waiting room where he was told to wait for the interviewer, who would be with him shortly. After what felt like a lifetime, the receptionist called Apollo in.

"She is ready to see you now," the receptionist said in a high-pitched, sing-song voice.

Apollo entered the office and instantly recognised the woman in front of him. His heart skipped a beat as he laid eyes on none other than the beautiful Alora from his high school days. Wow, he thought. He was speechless. Alora had blossomed into a fine young woman, and she smiled and put out her hand to introduce herself.

"Hi there," she began, "I am Alora Pollitis; thank you for coming to meet with me today," she said in her most professional voice. Apollo was mesmerised; he could not take his eyes off her. "Apollo, that's an unusual name," she remarked offhandedly. "Where are you from, may I ask?" Apollo was gobsmacked and disappointed; she hadn't recognised him at all. How could she have forgotten him?

"Ah, umm," he stammered nervously, unable to find the words. He took a deep breath, wondering in the back of his mind how she had managed to climb the ranks to interviewer status so fast; but he reminded himself to stay focused on the task at hand, because he really wanted this job.

"It's a Greek name, and I am from Cyprus," he explained slowly and deliberately, still finding it hard to believe she didn't know him. "But I've been living in Australia for seven years now," he said, never breaking eye contact with the woman before him.

"So, what made you want to apply for this position, and why do you feel you would be the best candidate for the job?" she quizzed him. This was painful. Apollo drew another breath.

"Well, I always wanted to get into the medical field; it is a passion of mine to work with people and help them, as I believe I have the heart and desire for it."

Alora smiled, impressed with his answer and went on to explain that he would have to fill out a questionnaire and that she could assist him with it. He also needed to pass a medical test and blood test, as required by all employees. Apollo nodded, still astonished that he had crossed paths with her again; his mind whizzed at a million miles an hour, as so many questions came to him now. He wished he could ask her why she left Moonee Ponds; where she went; why did her father take her out of the school? Was she married—? No, no, he thought, stopping himself; he couldn't possibly ask her that. Better to just stay professional, he reasoned.

Apollo finished the questionnaire, and Alora congratulated him on a job well done, inviting him to start work the following Monday. Apollo was excited, thrilled that he had been selected for the position but sad that Alora hadn't remembered him from four years earlier. Still, he thanked her for the offer of employment and gratefully accepted. Alora extended her hand and he took it firmly, grasping her slender, beautiful fingers he'd remembered from so long ago.

"Great! We shall see you here for your first day with us next Monday," Alora confirmed, still smiling.

"Thank you," Apollo replied, turning to leave. Alora giggled.

"My absolute pleasure, my Greek boy," she replied, winking.

My God! Apollo thought. *Boom! She remembers him!* Apollo was so shocked that, as he turned to leave, he walked headlong into the exit door, nearly tripping over himself. Alora laughed and clapped her hands as Apollo made a second hurried exit out the door. All the way home he had to keep pinching himself, because he just could not believe it was real. *What were the chances?* he thought. Apollo was not a betting man, but if he had been …

When Apollo arrived home, Natalie was calling him to the bedroom.

"Can you go out to the shops and get some groceries? I'm so exhausted after a full day with Jordan!" she cried. Apollo nodded quietly, putting his jacket back on.

"What's wrong?" she asked. "Did the interview not go well? Something's wrong—I can see it on your face. You know, people are asking if we are going to get married one day and have more kids, so tell me what's wrong," she demanded. But Apollo didn't dare tell her who had interviewed him, only that he'd got the job.

"Well, I must have had a great interview, because I got the job and I start next Monday and it's six months training and wages increase to twenty-five dollars an hour if I stay on," he said, grabbing the shopping list and walking out the door.

"So why so glum, then?" she called back, but by then, Apollo was already well on his way.

Apollo secretly couldn't wait for Monday; he wondered how it was going to work with Alora as his new boss, and how he was going to act around her and how he was going to keep this a secret from Natalie. He had made a promise to her that he would never see Alora again, but this was different; this was something that had been beyond his control; clearly, it had been left to the fate of the gods. At the crack of dawn, Apollo rose, showered and left; as he drove, he wondered about Alora, beautiful Alora, and he couldn't seem to get her out of his mind. He arrived at the facility, signed in, completed his induction and started his first training session, but Alora was nowhere to be seen.

In the afternoon Apollo was busy with a patient when finally Alora arrived with a little girl in tow.

"Hello, Apollo, this is my daughter, Emma," Alora announced, and the shy little four-year-old immediately hid behind her mother's skirt. Apollo was nervous too, but this little girl was the spitting image of Alora, and she was simply beautiful.

"I'm a single mother these days," Alora winked, "Which explains why my daughter has to come to work with Mummy sometimes, doesn't she?" she said, half speaking to Emma and scooping her up into her arms. Apollo was happy for Alora, but he felt sad hearing that she was doing it tough as a single mother. No woman deserved that, he thought, and he had to wonder how crazy a man would have to be to ever, ever give her up. Alora explained that her father had bought the company a few years back, which was why she was the head of the HR department, giving his daughter the day-to-day responsibilities of running it all.

"Well, you have done really well for yourself," Apollo replied, feeling awkward, suddenly not knowing what else to say. He couldn't believe a woman as beautiful as Alora could ever be single, but he had to think of Natalie and the baby and remain focused on his job, as hard as that was.

They did not say much after that, and each one separated to fulfill their work responsibilities. Before the day ended, however, Alora suddenly came rushing into the guest room where Apollo was feeding one of the residents. Even as he saw her out of the corner of his eye, Apollo's heart skipped a beat; the way her floral dress shimmied and sashayed as she walked, her very countenance affected him so. She was breathless.

"Apollo, your wife—" Alora began.

"You mean my partner," Apollo interrupted, quickly correcting her.

"Oh, well, she just called and, and, well I don't want to alarm you, but—"

"We aren't married," Apollo chimed in again, rather defensively.

"Oh—I'm sorry, well, your partner called us to inform you that your son was in an accident at creche today and has been rushed to the hospital," Alora said with some urgency. "And I have no problem at all with your leaving early, because I really think you should go," she said, wishing him well. Apollo's heart was in his throat, and he dropped what he was doing and raced to his car, forgetting to sign out; then he raced back inside again to ask which hospital.

"The Royal Children's Hospital—God speed to you, Apollo," Alora said, her voice trailing off.

"Thanks," Apollo said, dashing out the door.

Apollo raced into the hospital's reception area, asking where he could find his son and partner, and they redirected him to the Emergency Department's triage bay. Apollo sped down the hallway at lightning speed, where he ran into Natalie's parents as he rounded the corner.

"What happened?" he asked frantically.

"Natalie said that Jordan fell headfirst, after climbing onto a kitchen cupboard; he has been bleeding a lot and has lost fair amount of blood, so they need to find a match for his blood type, ASAP," Natalie's mother explained.

"That's fine, I will donate my blood right now—that's my son!" Apollo cried, distressed.

"Okay," the doctor said, approaching Apollo and figuring out who he was. "Follow me, we need to get you tested first to guarantee the match," he said, already at a fast clip down the hall to the haematology department. Apollo immediately had his blood drawn and tested, and was then told to wait in the waiting room until the doctor returned. Apollo sat quietly and waited; he had no idea where Natalie and Jordan were yet, but he took a moment and quietly prayed to God to keep them safe. Moments later the doctor returned with a dreadful look on his face.

"You say you are the father, is this correct?"

"Yes," Apollo said, thinking only of his son. The doctor frowned.

"I am so sorry, but going on the blood work and DNA samples we took, that little boy is not your son."

"Am I not the same blood type?" Apollo asked, confused. His eyes met with the doctor's stern look, and the doctor took the seat next to him. Now Apollo was shaking.

"Mr Mazarou," he said, gently placing his hand on Apollo's shoulder. Apollo shuddered. The doctor shook his head.

Apollo was thunderstruck; he felt as if he had just been squashed, crushed under a pile of bricks. His shock quickly turned to disbelief, then from disbelief to anger. He was infuriated.

Natalie came down the hall just at that moment, looking relieved. "It's okay, hun, I'm a suitable donor for Jordan," she smiled. The doctor looked from Apollo to Natalie and felt uneasy, suggesting they talk in private in one of the meeting rooms. But it was too late. Apollo raged at her.

"You lying fucking bitch! How dare you! You've ruined, ruined my life!" Apollo screamed murderously at Natalie, her eyes growing wide. All the nurses at the nurse's station immediately began hitting buttons, alerting the ward to a Code Two Grey. Apollo screamed again and it shook the pictures on the walls, sending the hospital staff into a panic. Natalie's father came over to Apollo to ask what the matter was.

"I am not the boy's father!" Apollo raged, out of control. "Jordan is not my son—your daughter has lied to me!" Natalie had just been blown out of the water now, and she knew it; she just couldn't believe she had just been exposed. Everything felt as though it was crumbling around them.

Apollo became emotional then, falling to his knees on the cold hospital floor in sheer desperation. Maybe the doctors had got it all wrong; maybe Apollo just needed to demand a new DNA test, and maybe this nightmare wasn't a nightmare at all but just a very bad mix up of blood work or test results or something. But when Apollo could finally bring himself to look across to Natalie for any sign of hope in her eyes, she just broke down too and started to cry, and then all Apollo could see in that moment was the fear behind her eyes, and it was a fear that looked just like Gavin Croosy, Simon Libb and Cale Moss. And that was the moment when Apollo finally learned the truth.

"You ruined my life, Natalie baby," he whispered, and left.

CHAPTER EIGHTEEN

Beyond the Ruins

"You cannot undo the past; you can only learn from it," Yiayia said kindly. "God will give you justice."

Apollo was distraught that the little boy he had come to love was not his own flesh and blood. How could Natalie do such a thing to him? She had finally come clean to Apollo, admitting that she'd also slept with Gavin Croosy of all people, and hadn't known who the father was. She said she'd guessed it had been Croosy, because the condom had broken, but in her panic, she had told Apollo he was the father because she would have rather have him than Croosy. Natalie had cried a thousand crocodile tears, but once Jordan was safely out of the hospital, Apollo quietly packed his bags and left despite her begging pleas to stay. There was no more anger, no hate or revenge left in Apollo; he'd been in the revenge business too long already, so instead he committed himself to work on forgiving her. But he just couldn't stay in something that was dead.

Apollo returned to live with his grandparents, where Yiayia and Frank were naturally devastated for their grandson; they knew they had to be strong for him now, and they continued to remind him that he was still so young and had so much life left to live.

"Let me tell you a little story, a Greek myth," Yiayia said, offering him soup for comfort. "Have you heard the story of Odysseus? If you've ever read the Greek poet Homer, who wrote *The Iliad* and *The Odyssey*. *The Odyssey* was about a young man, Odysseus, who goes off to fight in the Battle of Troy. You, my son, are in fact, Odysseus."

Yiayia raised her eyebrows as she leaned across and put down her tea.

"Anyway, the city of Troy would eventually be burned down, but on his journey, Odysseus meets with a lot of trouble along the way; he arrives on an island, waylaid and inhabited by Cyclops, who are big one-eyed giants and bullies—and they hate him and taunt him and want him killed because he's a hero and they're insanely jealous of him. Odysseus is the underdog; he knows he's not as strong as them, but he's crafty and good at everything and has multiple other talents, and he never gives up because he always finds a creative solution."

"Okay, I'm listening," Apollo remarked wryly.

"Well, in the final days when they are after him, Odysseus cleverly disguises himself as a pauper, a beggar and a swineherd (or pig shepherd) so that they won't recognise him and come after him. Pretty clever, huh? Until one day he goes in a contest to string his own bow, not realising that this will expose him—because only Odysseus can string a bow like that! This gives him away; suddenly they recognise he is Odysseus and try to kill him again. But Odysseus is now much stronger than before, because Athena, the good Goddess, helps to make him extra strong—so Odysseus gets his bow and fights back, finally killing them all. Being stuck amongst foreigners and not with his own peoples, Odysseus just wants to make it home again—because he never really wanted to leave his home anyway—so he leaves the island, having been nearly destroyed, and then runs into a goddess named Kirke; he is so enticed by the goddess and her wiles that he cannot see she is secretly a witch who is also out to destroy him. She switches his men and turns them into swine just as they are trying to make their way home (which makes it easy for them all to be killed, because now they are just lowly pigs who cannot fight back). It is only the good Goddess Athena, the goddess of wisdom who comes and tells him what he needs to know and is his true helper, while the other gods are all against him. Odysseus cries, because he trusted in someone when he shouldn't have, and he left his homeland when he never really wanted to; but that doesn't make him a fool, it just makes him mortal. What happens to Kirke is that she dies, so her due punishments do eventually come back to her in the end."

"Cute story," Apollo replied dryly. Yiayia shot him a knowing look. If anyone knew Apollo by now, she did, and she could interpret his sarcasm coming a mile off.

"Well, the Apollo I know is like Odysseus in many ways," Yiayia pressed on, "because he never wanted to leave home in the first place; just like me, he was forced out of his homeland in a cruel and unjust way—and then he was mocked and bullied, just like Odysseus was. Yet take a look at the facts here, and humour me if you will: he survived their torments, the mental torture and endless bullying. In his vulnerable state he was waylaid by the beautiful but deadly Natalie, who bewitched him and tricked him

… yet here he is— still here! He survives it all, because deep down he is strong, much stronger than he thinks, and really, in many ways he has already proven this by the simple fact that he is still here; he is still standing. He is a survivor. He just needs to believe in himself."

"All I've ever wanted was to love someone and be loved; yet most of the time it's just felt like I've been chasing the wind," Apollo admitted sadly, letting his guard down.

"I know, son, I know. In my own life I have faced similar moments of defeat. Being forced out of my homeland, away from my family and friends terrified me, crushed me, almost ruined me in ways you cannot understand—and back then I didn't even know if, or how, I was ever going to survive. I am still haunted today by the memories of my lost past, and I still yearn for the scent of the lemon trees, the land where my ancestors walked—but what I've come to realise is that it hasn't gone—it's never gone—because it lives, well, inside of me. Our memory is a funny thing, Apollo, because it likes to hold onto and remember pain, it never wants to let go. When the mind is supercharged, all it can think of and all it can see is division. And Cyprus has had decades of division. But just because the peace talks never worked over there, doesn't mean that they can't work here. Peace is always accessible, it is everywhere, it lives with us daily, it is in our backyards—we just have to choose it. I used to walk up to the tops of the hills in Cyprus and look out at all the ruins; it was such a sad sight, to see so much pointless destruction. Sometimes I could only see the ruins, and nothing else; and my mind would become clouded by anger, even hate, at the senselessness of it all. I hated the Turks for what they did to us, and I just couldn't see past it. Hate blinded me. But other times I would climb to the top of that hill, and right when I least expected it, I could see beyond the ruins; and I could see sky and cloud and water and light, and they would all marry together and make the most perfect story; and I could see too, how the light sometimes made it through the cracks of the ruins, and I thought about how stunning that looked, to see something so sad and broken become so beautiful, just like that."

Yiayia offered him a small plate of bourekia, Greek sweet pastries, and then she decided it was time to go, and as she got up her knees creaked, and she wobbled out the door in her slippers, wishing Apollo a good night.

Apollo thought about her words, her stories; he just wished his own story could be as perfect. He knew right now he was in the eye of the storm, but the evil eye would always protect him until one day when the storm would be over even though he knew he wouldn't be the same person as before. But wasn't that really the point of the storm, anyway? That, he knew, was what this storm was all about.

***

The weekend had come and gone in an instant for Apollo, but he had asked for a couple of days off to recharge. Now he realised he needed to take charge of his own life. He wrote a list of dos and don'ts to keep himself on track; he would make a conscious effort to maintain a healthier relationship with his mother and father, and he'd catch up with his brother Troy most weekends. He decided to work hard and save enough for a house deposit and stay single for a while and work on himself, give back to himself; he found a cute little flat in Fawkner, and as his bank account grew, he bought himself a puppy, a shepherd cross Labrador he named Lana. By 1994, Apollo had started living his own life. One day he was called into a meeting with Alora, who told him that he was doing an amazing job and that his hard work and his compassion and empathy for the residents had not gone unnoticed by the company. Apollo didn't know what to say, so he remained silent, humble, and grateful. Finally, she asked Apollo if he would meet her Friday night after work, but Apollo dismissed the idea pretty quickly.

"I really appreciate the gesture and all, Alora, but I have been through enough pain and heartache to last two lifetimes," he replied, looking into her azure blue eyes. It was hard to say no to her because he still loved her, but he'd been confused by her mind games and her pretending not to know him back when he'd started working there, and he was simply nobody's fool anymore; once bitten, twice shy, as they say. To be honest, after eight years Apollo had even had enough of Melbourne and its shortcomings, and had instead begun to fantasise about returning to a life in Cyprus. It was calling him back.

He spoke to Yiayia and Frank about the idea, and they were understandably sad, but they supported him, telling him it would do him good to have some time away, some time at home with his countrymen. He looked up some relatives, calling to see if there was any work in aged care and if they could put him up to stay, and then Apollo booked his one-way ticket to Cyprus. Then he had to break the news to Alora at work.

"Hey, I've got some news to tell—so I've decided to head home to Cyprus for a while, you know, to see my country and relatives and such," he announced hesitantly, thanking her for the job offer and the chance to grow in the industry.

"Wow, really?" Alora said, looking startled. "What brought this on?"

"Oh, you know, time to move on, and all that jazz," Apollo replied, trying to sound casual. He was a horrible liar.

"Umm, well when are you leaving?" she asked, trying to hide her sadness and disappointment.

"I booked a ticket for May 16th, two weeks from now—you know, so I could get organised and pack and stuff ..." he said, kicking at the rubber sole of his shoe. "Well, anyway, I best be off—thanks for everything, and I hope you and Emma stay well, and please keep in touch," he said, shaking her hand and wanting to leave things all businesslike between them. As he left, Alora could not help but be impressed by the man who'd just stood before her; Apollo was now of great stature and physique, and he held himself with a self-confidence assertiveness she had never seen before. It was a far cry from their high school days when he had once been so weak, meek and mild, she thought.

The day arrived and Apollo dropped off presents for his mother and father, Maggie, Troy, Yiayia, and Papou; he thanked them all for everything they had done for him and promised he would be in touch and visit soon, assuring them that this wasn't a goodbye; rather, it was just a temporary thing. In fact, he was excited to start afresh, because Yiayia was right; he was still young, and he had so much life left in him that now he didn't want to waste it. They arrived at the airport and said a teary goodbye in the way large Greek families are known to do.

"I'm gonna miss you, bro," Troy said first, tears welling in his dark Greek eyes. They embraced in a tight bear hug before Apollo turned and saw his gate was open; he gave Yiayia one last kiss then turned to leave through the terminal when a voice behind him came out of nowhere, screaming. All he could hear was, "Apollo! Wait! Wait!"

He turned around to see who was calling his name, and beyond the ruins there she was, waiting.

Alora ran past security and pulled Apollo in close. "Wait, wait—" she gasped, catching her breath. She put her hand over his mouth then, stopping Apollo from being able to speak. "Wait, please, hear me out—I need to tell you how much I love you, Apollo. You can't leave me now!" Alora cried. "I have loved you from the minute we met—and I have never, ever stopped loving you. I love the way you squeeze lemon on everything; I love the way your nose crinkles up when you disagree with something; I love the loyalty you have to your family; I love your soft eyes and kind heart, your peace loving spirit; I love the way you run like the wind and put up a fight, and never, ever give up—and I love your Greekness, how you stay the same, no matter what, or who, or where you are. We have been through so much, Apollo—and I too have made mistakes, but I have to tell you something: I fell pregnant that night you and I were caught in the basement in the fire—when we made love—and I haven't been with anyone since. Emma is your daughter, Apollo. My father was ashamed of me and took me out of school and away from you because in his eyes I had dishonoured the Greek village and had broken tradition. But, my God, Apollo, I love you so much. Please don't leave me again. I just couldn't bear losing you a second time around." Alora was speaking so fast now that Apollo was in a state of shock as the words flew by him, around him, in him, and it stirred all kinds of feelings deep within that sent his head spinning and his heart reeling from the news Alora had just hit him with. He looked at Alora, and found himself completely speechless.

"Please don't leave; I saw your name in the application pile, and it was my way of keeping you close, of bringing you back into my life. Please come back to me, Apollo; everything is different now. Nothing—nothing—is ruined."

Apollo looked across to his grandparents for guidance, because he simply didn't trust his own instincts anymore. Yiayia stood there and watched on with tears in her eyes, finally giving her grandson the look of approval.

"Go on, mana mou; go with your one true love; go be with her and be happy, because God always has his hand on you, no matter what."

Apollo turned to look at the terminal and then back at Alora, before instinctively taking her in his arms. "I never stopped loving you, Alora. I have been betrayed before; just tell me, how do I know this child is mine?"

Alora grabbed her bag and pulled out the papers with Emma's DNA on it.

"How did you get this?" he said, now looking truly stunned.

"After your work medical, I had your blood work analysed because I needed the proof; please, I know this is hard for you—I wanted to find you and tell you everything so long ago, but I was forced by my father, made to promise I would never see you again. But in my heart I vowed to find you, and I knew that one day we would find our way back to each other. I cannot offer you much; this is all that I am, Apollo, but I hope that this is enough for you, and I can only pray to God that you feel the same way too."

"Is this man my Daddy?" Emma asked softly, coming out now from behind her mother's skirt. Alora looked for a sign of hope in Apollo's eyes. When she found it, she answered her daughter.

"Yes he, is, darling."

"As you wish," Apollo smiled, scooping his daughter up in his arms.

EPILOGUE

After the End

"I know this is the way to live now, beyond the ruins, beyond the rubble of my past hurts, of all the things that have held me back. I can lie underneath the ruins and remain the once broken soul I was, or I can hear the whisperings of the Gods, see the dappled light as it comes shining through the cracks, leading me the way out of darkness, and into the light," Apollo told the sensei, thanking him for everything he had taught him.

"Yes, my child; I can see how much you have grown— you are now well on your way to mastering the art of self-perfection, and becoming a Karateka, the caretaker of your own soul, for this is where the riches are to be found."

Apollo would go on to study for three years, finally obtaining his degree in nursing and medical science; he would then buy Alora a ring and propose in a treasure hunt that drew them out to sea. They would be married in Cyprus and stay in the Greek islands for two weeks, travelling around on their honeymoon and taking in all the sights. When he had enough money saved, Apollo and Alora would buy a house in Moonee Ponds, not far from Yiayia and Frank. Sadly, Papou would pass away at the ripe old age of eighty-seven, to go play backgammon in the sky, while Yiayia would continue to stay healthy and well, surrounded by the love of her family. Every year Apollo and Alora made a point to return to Cyprus and spend a month reconnecting with relatives and their native homeland, though times were busy what with three children in tow, as Alora would give birth to a set of fraternal twins they named Helen and Noah.

Apollo, named after the sun god Apollo in ancient Greece, now proudly celebrates his name day on September 3rd, a date he shares with his mother Mary's birthday. Mary is a now a nurse and works in pathology, and every year on their birthdays they get together for a big party, sharing in a great big feast together, with Mary ever the doting grandmother to all her grandchildren. Troy would go on to marry a wonderful woman, Sophie, and they would have three beautiful daughters together; Jaydah, Emily and Sophia. Mateus would beat a cancer scare and, though newly retired, remains married to Olivia and has a healthy relationship with both Apollo and Troy. He loves fishing and Greek music and going out to the Greek Cyprus Cafe Club on Friday and Saturday nights, as an integral member of the Melbourne Greek community.

Alan would die tragically of cancer after a motorbike accident's scans revealed the terminal growth, and little sister Maggie would grow up to marry an Aussie guy who works in construction. Apollo occasionally sees Natalie and Jordan around the traps, and they share a polite and courteous hello, because you know, that's just the way the wind blows; it keeps blowing around the world, because the past will always keep reinventing itself, beyond the ruins.

God Will Give Me Justice
—The Count of Monte Cristo

They shall build up the ancient ruins;
they shall raise up the former devastations;
they shall repair the ruined cities, the devastations
of many generations.
Strangers shall stand and tend your flocks;
foreigners shall be
your plowmen and vinedressers.
—Isaiah 61:1-8

*What you have inherited from your fathers, work on,
that you may possess it.*
—Goethe

www.ingramcontent.com/pod-product-compliance
Lightning Source LLC
Chambersburg PA
CBHW031245290426
44109CB00012B/449